HONDA
GOLD WING
THE COMPLETE STORY

Other Titles in the Crowood MotoClassics Series

HONDA GOLD WING

THE COMPLETE STORY

PHIL WEST

The Crowood Press

First published in 2003 by
The Crowood Press Ltd
Ramsbury, Marlborough
Wiltshire SN8 2HR

www.crowood.com

British Library Cataloguing-in-Publication Data
A catalogue record for this book is available from the British Library.

ISBN 1 86126 584 0

Typeset by Servis Filmsetting Ltd, Manchester

Printed and bound in Great Britain by Bookcraft, Midsomer Norton

Contents

The very first GL1000K1 Gold Wing as unveiled to a bemused motorcycling press at the 1974 IFMA Cologne Motor Show. Biking journalists weren't quite sure what to make of its liquid-cooled, flat four-cylinder engine, underseat fuel tank and elephantine (for the times) dimensions.

Introduction

There's a certain irony in the claim that the Honda Gold Wing is more than a mere motorcycle. At the launch of the original, the GL1000 in 1974, the world's press were both stunned and sceptical. Here was a monstrous machine that, while not as technically innovative as Honda would have liked us to believe, was most certainly a bold concept. For the first time, car met motorcycle. Unprecedented long-distance comfort was offered to the rider, however a car-like bulk and manners were a frequent criticism.

As a result it was no overnight success story, but the twenty-six years of continuous production since with five major model updates and sales of over 500,000 tells a rather different story.

And what a story. The original Gold Wing, taking its name from Honda's traditional emblem, may have created a stir, but it went on to create a phenomenon. The creation of the GL1100 Interstate in 1981, the first Gold Wing to be equipped with a full fairing, panniers, top box and optional stereo, all for a suggested retail price of $4,898, represented the birth of the 'full-dress tourer'. It was a class of machine that became hugely popular, especially in the USA, a market segment the Gold Wing has dominated ever since despite numerous jealous rivals. The Interstate immediately won accolades from the enthusiast press, praise that translated into healthy sales figures. *Cycle World* magazine named the GL1100 Interstate its Best Touring Bike for 1980, an honour the motorcycle (and its sub-sequent variants) retained for eleven consecutive years.

And the machines themselves kept getting better. The GL1100 begat the GL1200 and subsequently the GL1200 Aspencade – fuel injection, travel computer and all. The GL1200 led to the wondrous six-cylinder GL1500, which re-wrote the full-dresser rules, a machine so dominant that it remained in production, virtually unchanged, for nearly thirteen years.

And now there is the aluminium-framed GL1800. The Gold Wings of today are the motorcycling equivalent of the Winnebago motorhome. These huge, lavishly equipped juggernauts are designed to carry large American gentlemen and their even larger wives from coast to coast with music on the stereo and every item of clothing they possess stowed in the panniers and top box. The latest six-cylinder GL1800 produces 118bhp at 5,500rpm, more torque than any motorcycle ever made, weighs 792lb (360kg) without liquids, requires a 1,100watt alternator to power its zillion plug-in accessories and appears to have been built to withstand a direct hit from a cruise missile!

And perhaps that's appropriate, as it would probably take just that to dislodge the Wing from its position as king of tourers. Today, the Gold Wing (the Honda part of the name is unnecessary) is blessed with one of the most loyal customer followings found anywhere in motorcycling – nine out of ten Gold Wing owners would buy another. A huge club scene exists and with it camaraderie only Harley can rival.

This book attempts to chronicle and explain the emergence, development and growth of the Gold Wing legend where it counts the most – the machines themselves. But it is not just an exhaustive technical essay. I've striven to unearth the men and the minds behind the machines wherever possible, in the process uncovering many never previously published photographs, which will, I hope, paint a more colourful and comprehensive picture of the Wing than has been done before.

This has been a journey of discovery worthy of the Gold Wing itself and would not have been possible without the help and support of my wife, Fiona, and family; assistance from Honda in the UK, USA and Japan and the inspiration of my father, Lawrence West. I remember seeing my first GL1000 in his motorcycle showroom in 1975. I never imagined it would lead to this . . .

Key Dates

1906	Birth of Soichiro Honda
1922	Honda leaves school to work as a mechanic
1928	Motor repair business established
1937	Foundation of Honda's first company, Tokai Seiki Heavy Industry (TSHI)
1942	*Toyo Kogyo* (Toyota Motor Co.) buys 40 per cent of TSHI
1945	Honda sells his remaining 60 per cent of TSHI to *Toyo Kogyo*
1946	Honda establishes the Honda Technical Research Institute in Hamamatsu
1947	First Honda product, the A-type bicycle engine
1948	Honda Motor Company Ltd founded
1949	First Honda motorcycle, the 98cc two-stroke Dream
1950	Tokyo sales branch founded
1951	Dream Type E four-stroke 146cc motorcycle launched
1952	Cub 50cc scooter (Type F) launched
1953	Benly 90cc motorcycle (Type J) launched
	Honda releases its first Power Product engine
1954	Juno 200cc scooter (Type K) launched
	Soichiro Honda visits Isle of Man TT Races for the first time
	Juno scooter exported to USA
1957	Honda R&D centre set up
	Dream C-70 250cc four-stroke motorcycle launched
1958	Super Cub motorbike launched
1959	Honda racing team takes sixth place in 125cc class at Isle of Man TT Races
	American Honda Motor Co., Inc. founded in Los Angeles
1960	First overseas production facility founded in Taiwan
1961	Advertising campaign 'You Meet the Nicest People on a Honda' launched
	Honda sweeps first three places in Isle of Man TT Races
	European Honda GmbH (now Honda Deutschesland GmbH) founded in Hamburg
1962	S500, Honda's first sports car, launched in Japan
	Suzuka racing circuit completed
1963	Honda competes in Formula 1 Grand Prix racing for the first time
	Honda Benelux NV (Belgium) begins motorcycle production
1964	S600 roadster sports car launched
	Honda France SA (Paris) established
1965	S600 roadster exported for the first time

	Records first F1 victory in Mexico (1500cc)
	Honda UK Ltd established in London
1966	Wins manufacturer's championship in all Grand Prix classes (50cc, 125cc, 250cc, 350cc and 500cc) – a first
1967	Wins F1 Grand Prix in Italy (3000cc)
1968	Ten-millionth Honda two-wheeler is built, a CB450 'Black Bomber', and is ridden off the production line by Soichiro Honda himself
	CB750 launched
1970	CB750 wins Daytona 200
1972	Honda Civic car launched
1973	Soichiro Honda and Takeo Fujisawa retire, Kiyoshi Kawashima becomes President of Honda Motor
1974	Honda Gold Wing GL1000 motorcycle launched
1976	Honda Accord car launched
1977	Honda Civic car ranks first in USA fuel economy tests for fourth consecutive year
1978	Honda Prelude car launched
1979	Honda of America Manufacturing opens and begins motorcycle assembly
1980	Groundbreaking for an automobile plant in Ohio
1981	Honda wins 500cc motocross world title for third consecutive year
1983	Honda returns to Formula 1 racing after a fifteen-year hiatus
1986	Legend V6 luxury saloon launched
1987	US-built Accord cars and Gold Wing motorcycles imported to Japan for the first time
1989	Soichiro Honda becomes the first Asian to be inducted into USA Automotive Hall of Fame
	Accord becomes the best-selling car in the USA
1990	The NSX, a new sports car, launched
	Honda wins the J. D. Power Consumer Satisfaction Index for fifth consecutive year
1991	Tenth consecutive win in Isle of Man TT Races
	Death of Soichiro Honda
1993	Honda Dream wins World Solar Challenge
1994	Honda enters Indy Car World Series
1995	Launch of the Honda Valkyrie, a new US-assembled custom motorcycle
	Honda wins Indy Car Manufacturers' Championship
1997	100-millionth two-wheeler produced
1999	Honda Motor Co, Inc. celebrates its fiftieth anniversary
2000	New $440 million auto plant near Lincoln, Alabama
	S2000 roadster launched

1 A History of Honda

It is just over fifty years since founder Soichiro Honda set up a business bolting tiny engines to bicycle frames. In this time, the Honda Motor Company has risen to become not just the world's largest motorcycle manufacturer but a major international corporation, ranked twenty-second in the world, with a turnover of more than $40 billion.

Honda is best known for motorcycles, and with good reason. With an annual production of over five million machines, it is by far the world's largest manufacturer of powered two-wheelers and is also the world leader in terms of product diversity, technical innovation and sporting activity.

While maintaining a dominant position in the motorcycle world, Honda has also become a major car manufacturer and greatly expanded its power product range and output. In fact, despite being the world leader, nowadays the bikes represent only a tiny proportion of Honda's business. Currently just 10 per cent of Honda's production capacity is devoted to two-wheelers and the whole motorcycle division generates only 1 per cent of the company's profits. But each of these three main areas of production, linked by their shared reliance on sophisticated engine technology, has played an important part in the company's growth in recent years.

In 1997 the company celebrated a unique record by producing its 100-millionth powered two-wheeler. Of these, over twenty-six million have been of the Super Cub series – characterized by its 'step-thru' design, con-venience and reliability – which revolution-ized personal transport on its launch in 1958 and has since become the world's best-selling powered vehicle of all time.

Although the company's early rise was based on small-capacity machines, Honda has long-produced bikes for all the main product sectors plus numerous niche markets. The most important large-capacity model in Honda's history was probably the four-cylin-der CB750 of 1969, which became known as the first 'superbike' and established the format that remains most popular for larger machines.

Honda's bikes have featured a wide variety of powerplants – arguably more than any other manufacturer. The number of cylinders alone has varied between one and the six of behe-moths like the CBX1000 of 1978 and the now legendary GL1500 Gold Wing.

In more recent years, Honda has made the V4 engine layout its own, producing a variety of roadsters ranging from the hugely success-ful VFR750 and 800 series to the Magna customs. V4s also powered the weird and wonderful NR750 of 1992, which was pro-duced as a showcase for Honda technology with 'oval' pistons and eight valves per cylin-der. Two-stroke technology has not been neglected either – the NSR500 V4 domi-nated 500cc Grand Prix racing during the 1990s, taking Aussie Mick Doohan to four consecutive world championships. Nowa-days, the all-new V5 RC11V four-stroke Moto GP machine has taken over the NSR's role.

The CB750 Four, launched in 1968 was unlike anything that had been seen before, from Japan or anywhere else.

The 1978 six-cylinder CBX1000 was a worthy successor to the CB750 and GL1000 Gold Wing.

Only Honda would have dared produce the NR750. As well as its stunning styling (which heavily influenced the Ducati 916) and cutting-edge chassis, there was an oval-pistoned engine.

The NR750's V4 engine boasted 'oval' pistons and two con-rods per piston. It was effectively a V8 but with pairs of pistons stuck together to make it a V4 in order to side-step Grand Prix racing rules.

The process of continual refinement has also kept Honda supersport machines such as the CBR900RR FireBlade and the phenomenally successful CBR600F at the top of their respective classes.

Honda is not only Japan's youngest car manufacturer, it is also now the nation's third largest (behind Toyota and Nissan) with an annual output of over two million vehicles.

The company diversified into four-wheeled production in the early 1960s and quickly gained a reputation for practical, well-designed vehicles with a distinctive style and superior engineering, such as the S600 sports car, lightweight cars such as the Life and Civic, and small vans. The latest Civic and the more recent Accord are best-sellers, remain popular

Australian Mick Doohan, five times 500cc world champion aboard the mighty Honda NSR500 V4.

Honda's NSR500 V4 Grand Prix machine of 1997. Arguably the most developed and dominant Grand Prix racing machine of all time.

worldwide and incorporate advanced technical features such as VTEC variable valve timing, four-wheel steering and traction control.

The Power Products division has long been an important part of Honda, having grown rapidly since it was established in 1953. Since then the range of output has broadened to include industrial machinery and a wide variety of equipment for recreational and leisure use.

The Honda Motor Company was founded by Soichiro Honda in October 1946. Known at first as the Honda Technical Research Institute, the company operated from a small wooden shed with just ten employees. Honda could see a huge demand for affordable, powered two-wheelers in war-scarred Japan and obtained a batch of 500 small petrol engines that he attached to bicycles. They were such a success that when the first batch of engines had been used up, he continued by making his own which were basically copies of the bought-in 50cc two-strokes. The new bike was officially called the Model A and the first example was produced in November 1947.

As production of Model A continued, Honda decided that the original name of his new company was now inappropriate and so renamed it the Honda Motor Company in September 1948.

The power output of the bikes was increased, first to 90cc (Model B) and then to 3bhp (Model C). The frames, however, were still bought in. Honda felt that both engine and frame should be made in-house to justify carrying his name on their sides. This plan was

The first headquarters of the fledgling Honda Motor Company in Hamamatsu in the early 1950s.

The Model A of 1947–51, progenitor of the whole Honda dynasty.

The Type F of 1952, called the 'Cub' to suggest friskiness and freedom, was an immediate success.

August 1949, the first prototype of the Dream Model D.

realized in August 1949 with the completion of his prototype for the Model D. The machine represented many firsts. It was the first Japanese motorcycle to be entirely the product of one manufacturer. It was also the first chain-driven Honda, powered by a two-stroke engine via a two-speed transmission with a sturdy pressed-steel frame and the latest type of telescopic fork front suspension. It was also the first Honda to carry the 'Dream' model name.

At this point, a second powerful figure in the development of the Honda Motor Company came on the scene. Soichiro Honda was undoubtedly the driving force during the early years (*see* Chapter 2) but we must also remember Takeo Fujisawa. The two had met in Tokyo in August 1949 and Fujisawa joined the fledgling company the following October. His role was to complement Honda's imaginative genius with a hard-headed grasp of finance. Fujisawa's expertise was not engineer-

ing, like Honda – but marketing. His first job was distribution. At the time he joined the company, Honda's products were only sold through around 200 outlets in the local Hamamatsu area. Under Fujisawa this quickly increased to 5,000 covering the whole of Japan. An office was opened in Tokyo, which was rapidly emerging from the ashes of the war to become Japan's economic centre in place of Osaka. This was followed by a new factory at Kami-jujo in the north of the city.

Although no engineer, Fujisawa had valuable ideas about products and commented to Honda one day about the unpleasant 'bata-bata' noise made by two-stroke bikes – he preferred the sound made by four-stroke machines and was convinced most customers did too. Soon after, the company started work on its first four-stroke design, which was to become the Model E. The first test run of the prototype was on July 15 1951 and was a

At that time, Honda sold both engines and complete motorcycles to distributors, and the Dream D was less popular than putting a Honda engine in a competitor's frame. Honda's business partner, Takeo Fujisawa, told distributors that if they wanted to sell the Dream, they could no longer get engines; if they wanted engines, they could not get the Dream. Such tactics angered some of the distributors so much that they allegedly threatened Fujisawa with knives!

Honda's first machine, the Model A, was essentially a bicycle to which a bought-in 50cc engine was attached.

resounding success. Production started soon afterwards at the Tokyo plant and Honda stuck solidly with this form of power for the next twenty years.

1952 was a significant year for Honda. This was the year that exports began, first to Okinawa, then to the Philippines. In addition, a second Tokyo plant was opened, this time at Shirako. In November of that year, Honda and Fujisawa travelled to Europe and the USA to look at manufacturing processes and buy machine tools – they were amazed at what they saw. They quickly realized they had to invest heavily in modern tools to improve both quality and production rates, and this was to become a cornerstone of the company's modus operandi.

March 1954 saw Honda's first official entry in a foreign motorcycle race. It was a somewhat inauspicious start, finishing thirteenth out of twenty-two in a Brazilian event. Honda and Fujisawa travelled to Europe once again, this time visiting the UK for the first time. Their purpose was to study the competition and the machinery at the Isle of Man TT Races and they came away convinced that Europe required a reliable, mass-market small bike and determined that Honda would be competing at the TT Races within five years. Knowing that racing success would be the key to worldwide sales, Honda was determined to match – and better – the high standards of engineering he had seen in action.

That first resolution was fulfilled with the Super Cub 100 of 1958, better known as the Honda 50. This went on to become probably the most significant road vehicle ever produced – right up there with the Volkswagen Beetle, Model T Ford and BMC Mini. Certainly in terms of sheer volume, the Super Cub series of scooterettes has outsold every other powered transport vehicle ever made.

The design brief was simple – basic transport for anyone who knows nothing about

1958 C100 Super Cub. Arguably the most important machine in the whole history of motorcycling, having outsold every other powered transport vehicle ever made.

motorcycles. There would be three gears, but with an automatic clutch. It had to be a proper vehicle with adequate lights and brakes so that it could be used on any type of road. Moreover, it was specifically designed to be neither motorcycle nor scooter and the terms 'scooterette' and 'step-thru' were born.

Large-diameter wheels and ample seating offered comfort comparable with larger touring motorcycles. Also, the automatic clutch meant that anybody who had never controlled a powered vehicle before could quickly master the Cub. And the 'step-thru' format created a fun two-wheeler, easily ridden by people of all ages and both sexes.

It was later offered in 70cc and 90cc forms and is still in demand today. The Super Cub may seem as far removed from the Gold Wing as is imaginable, but without it Honda, and the Gold Wing, would never have survived.

The company's first twin-cylinder machine, the 250cc C70, came in 1957. Honda had wanted to produce a more powerful machine and had settled on multiple cylinders, as opposed to both larger capacity or higher revving singles, both of which are inherently more stressed, as the best way of delivering it. The C70 also had a pressed-steel frame, the norm for Honda at that time, and a light alloy engine.

The following year, the C70 became the C71 with the addition of an electric starter and in January 1959 it was put on display at a leading motorcycle show in Amsterdam. It was the first Japanese machine that many people had ever seen and was the start of the opening of the European market for Honda – however, the real glittering prize was the USA.

In 1959, most US motorcycle sales were to enthusiasts who wanted large displacement home-grown machines such as Harley-Davidson and Indian or imported big British twins mainly from BSA, Triumph and Norton. When Honda of America was founded, the company's range of modern,

high-quality machines had the smaller engine capacity market virtually all to itself. Honda had recognized that the enthusiast market was not the only one: people who were not enthusiasts but who required reliable, two-wheeled transport would choose its C100 Super Cub, while those who were enthusiasts but who did not necessarily want to spend every waking moment immersed in old engine oil would choose the bigger C71 or even C75 and C76 models with increased displacements of 305cc.

As a result, in just a few years Honda was a dominant force on the world market – particularly in the all-important USA where, largely thanks to its amazingly successful advertising campaign 'You meet the nicest people on a Honda', it was by far the biggest seller of small motorcycles. Output from its plants reached a record 100,000 a month in 1961 and profits were ploughed back into expanding research facilities and diversifying the product range. This enabled the company to tailor its models to suit demands in various markets and during that year a European headquarters was established in Germany.

The time had now come for Honda to capture the attention of the full-bore motorcycle enthusiast too, and this was to be done through racing success and the production of new sophisticated models. The first part of this strategy was achieved at the Isle of Man TT Races in 1961 where Honda swept into the first three places in both the 125 and 250cc classes. Grand Prix success was soon to follow.

The first sportsbikes, aimed at the European enthusiast market, were also on the way. First of all came the CB71, subsequently updated to the CB72 (or Hawk in the USA). The impact of the 250cc twin-cylinder CB72 made it the most talked about motorcycle in Europe and the USA. The power from its free-revving engine was a revelation to riders who had only ever experienced such performance from big, heavy machines that were often awkward, oily

The Pico Building, Los Angeles, headquarters of the American Honda Motor Company, Inc., founded in 1959.

and unreliable. And it was a superb introduction to the pleasures of motorcycling for masses of young novices. With its compact all-tubular chassis, telescopic fork front suspension and reliable 12-volt electrics, the CB72's many admirers included some anxious European manufacturers.

Then, in 1963, the CB77 (or Super Hawk in the USA) was introduced. This was basically a CB72 but with a bigger bore to take it up to 305cc and the power up from 24 to 27.5bhp. These figures may not be much by modern standards, but back then it was enough to

make the CB77 more than a match for any contemporary 500cc British twin.

An outstanding feature of all early Honda sportsbikes was their brakes – full-width large-diameter alloy hubs incorporating cast-iron drums and housing twin leading shoe backplates. Contemporary European machines had nothing to rival this. Honda was moving up – fast.

This was a period of massive and ambitious expansion for the company, which ended up transforming the whole of the motorcycling world. European manufacturing began in

To spearhead its push into the USA with the C100 Super Cub, Honda came up with a brilliantly successful advertising campaign, which also improved the image of motorcyclists. Its slogan? The now legendary 'You meet the nicest people on a Honda'.

The 1960 CB72 enabled many riders to enjoy their motorcycling to the full, whether simply touring or competing in endurance races.

It was also known as the 'Hawk' in the USA. Small bike, big performance.

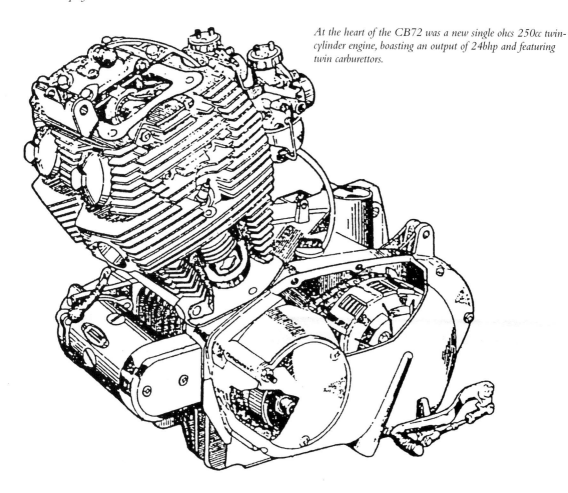

At the heart of the CB72 was a new single ohcs 250cc twin-cylinder engine, boasting an output of 24bhp and featuring twin carburettors.

1963 with the production of mopeds at the Honda Benelux facility in Belgium. European centres were also set up in France and the UK, and the Asian Honda Motor Co. was established in Thailand. Sales in the USA had reached a market-leading 150,000 motorcycles. But did the European manufacturers take note?

By 1965 Honda had pulled clear of every other make in both production and exports and a succession of new products was being devised, not only to meet market demands, but to create new types of leisure motorcycles.

Unbelievably, European manufacturers continued to bury their heads in the sand. The contemporary wisdom was that the market was divided into two – those who required basic transport and enthusiasts. But the real profits, it was believed, were in large-capacity sportsbikes bought by older, more experienced riders. Customers, they thought, would tend to upgrade from small bikes to larger ones as they matured. As the Japanese did not make any large bikes, they concluded that the Japanese were actually doing them a favour by introducing more young people to motorcycling, leaving the field clear for them to concentrate on big sportsbikes with their associated big profits. All of that would have been fine – if Honda had not thought of it first and formulated its own plans to take the big bike market by storm.

When Honda made a shock entry to the larger capacity league in 1966, it did so in a typically original way. The company's first 500cc-class bike, the CB450 of 1965, had an entirely new twin-cylinder engine with double ohcs – a layout until then associated with only the most exotic works racing motorcycles and cars. The CB450 also featured a most unusual type of valve spring, not coiled but in the form of a torsion bar, activated by being twisted along its length.

Despite the advanced specification and 100mph (161km/h) capability, the Black Bomber, as it was nicknamed, also proved manageable and easy to ride. On its cubic capacity alone the CB450 was an industry milestone. The old-established makers had believed Honda would be content to concentrate on smaller entry-level machines for the sports market. Now they were suddenly faced

Briton Mike 'the bike' Hailwood, arguably Honda's most famous rider during the 1960s and the winner of countless world championships for the company.

Launched in 1965, the CB450 evolved out of the CB77, the 305cc supersport model of the Dream series. The CB450 became known for peaky power delivery typical of high-revving racing engines, calling for frequent gear changes. Following the advice of Honda USA it was decided that a model with flatter torque characteristics and a larger cubic capacity was needed. It was also deemed necessary that the new bike should offer better performance than any British or US models. Thus was born the concept of Honda's four-cylinder CB750.

by Honda's mission to bring its standards of quality and refinement to the experienced rider of larger capacity machines.

But probably the single most dramatic expression of Honda's desire to take on the 'big boys' was the astonishing CB750 Four. When it was unveiled at the 1968 Tokyo Motor Show this dazzling four-cylinder bike represented one of the greatest technical leaps since motorcycling began. Until then there had only been a handful of four-cylinder motorcycles and none had offered the power, sophistication and availability represented by the CB750. Not only did it boast a potent ohc engine, the big Four also outpaced everything else in its class by offering a disc front brake and a five-speed gearbox as well as the usual Honda features such as an electric starter and an excellent finish.

Able to top 120mph (193km/h) but docile at city speeds, the CB750 delivered its power more smoothly than any big sportster that had gone before. It was, without question, the world's first superbike, having proved its mettle by winning France's *Bol d'Or* 24-hour race in 1969 and the 1970 Daytona 200 in the USA.

By 1970, Honda's range covered everything from mopeds to high-powered superbikes, and by setting up local production facilities it was able meet the particular demands of different regions. Plants in Brazil and Mexico were followed in 1979 by the establishment of Honda of America, built to make the Gold Wing at Marysville, Ohio.

Having established four-cylinder credentials with the CB750, Honda undertook the tricky

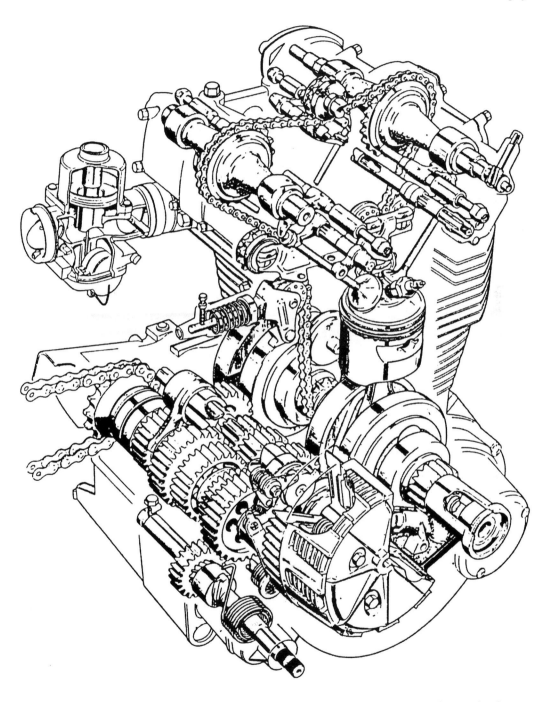

A first for volume-produced motorcycles, the double ohcs twin-cylinder engine of the CB450 was based on Honda's client racer engines, with torsion bar valve springs able to withstand 10,000rpm. To produce a 450cc engine that would surpass the performance of the popular British ohv 650cc vertical twin demanded maximum use of advanced technology.

The CB750 made its
world debut at the
1968 Tokyo Motor
Show and caused a
sensation.

Honda had two 750 Four prototypes ready for the 1968 Tokyo Motor Show – a drum-braked version that had already featured in Japanese motorcycle magazines, and a machine fitted with a disc front brake still undergoing development. When he came to look over the show stand, Soichiro Honda was asked which bike should be displayed. Always a man to promote innovation, he answered: 'Obviously you should display the version with the disc brake'! And so the world's first commercially produced motorcycle to be equipped with a disc brake made its public debut.

Not only Honda fans greeted the mass-produced CB750: its reasonable cost and excellent quality made it popular amongst bike enthusiasts worldwide.

The CB750 pictured here is en route to victory in the hands of Michel Rougerie in the prestigious 1969 Bol d'Or 24-hour endurance race.

Another victory for the CB750, this time at America's flagship event, the Daytona 200 in March 1970. Dick Mann is riding here.

Aside from Dick Mann, Honda also engaged star riders Tommy Robb (left) and Ralph Bryans for the 1970 Daytona 200 race.

business of making the layout work as effectively in smaller engine sizes. The compact CB500F half-litre Four of 1971 immediately impressed with its smoothness, comfort and reliability, proving capable of brisk touring even two-up. With a top speed of over 110mph (177km/h), the reasonably priced 500 fitted the bill admirably for many sporting riders of the early 1970s.

The cute CB350F launched on some markets proved that a four-cylinder engine could be successfully scaled down even further. Though not hugely powerful, the neat little Four brought previously undreamed of smoothness and effortless revs to the medium-weight category.

More followed – inexorably. The CB400F of 1974 was a masterpiece of subtle styling that was an instant hit and drew many more enthusiasts to the marque. The little Four led a trend towards uncluttered, European-style 'cafe racer' machines. It had the lean looks of a competition bike with decals replacing badges on the tank, attractive and simple primary colour schemes, but the crowning glory was its four-into-one exhaust system.

Having established its four-cylinder credentials with the CB750, Honda undertook the tricky business of making the layout work as effectively in a number of smaller sizes. The CB500F of 1971 immediately impressed with its smoothness, comfort and reliability.

That a four-cylinder engine could be scaled down even further was shown by Honda's cute CB350F. Though not immensely powerful, the neat little four brought previously undreamed of smoothness and effortless revs to the medium weight category.

Meanwhile, every manufacturer's world title in road racing had been won and the 1970s brought new conquests in motocross, endurance racing and trials. A return to Grand Prix road racing in the 1980s saw Honda reclaim the 500cc title in 1983 and gradually attain the Grand Prix supremacy it still holds today.

Honda's cumulative motorcycle production over these fifty years has exceeded an amazing 100 million and the company now has four major world divisions: Japan, the Americas, Asia and Europe. The European motorcycle headquarters is in Rome with three factories in the region: a plant at Atessa builds the NX650 Dominator, Transalp and CB500 along with lightweights. Montesa Honda in Spain produces lightweights, scooters, the Deauville and the SLR650, and a plant has been recently established in Turkey.

The CB400F was an instant hit – a masterpiece of subtle styling that drew many enthusiasts to Honda for the first time when it was unveiled in 1974.

Furthermore, an astonishing variety of bikes have been produced – over 950 different models, ranging from electric power-assisted bicycles to fully equipped luxury tourers of 1520cc. Since Honda's creation in 1948, its rise has been nothing short of meteoric – no other motor company has achieved so much in just fifty years.

The NSX supercar boasts the world's most compact and powerful V6 powerplant, yet the car is also comfortable and practical.

Honda Facts and Figures

Listed below is some fun trivia spanning Honda's fifty years in the motorcycle industry, ranging from Honda history and innovations to racing to production.

- The first product to be sold displaying the Honda name was the 1947 A-type, a 50cc two-stroke making 1bhp at 5,000rpm. This was fitted to a standard bicycle frame and sold until 1951.
- In 1950, 2,633 motorcycles were sold in Japan. Of those, 1,000 were Hondas.
- In 1966, Honda captured all five Grand Prix manufacturers' championships.
- In 1970, Honda won the Daytona 200 in its first attempt with a CB750-based racer ridden by Dick Mann.
- The first motorcycle to roll off Honda's US assembly line at MMP, Ohio was the 1979 CR250R.
- Honda's NSR500 GP racer won six consecutive world championships from 1994 to 1999 in the hands of Mick Doohan and then Alex Criville, including twenty-two consecutive race wins between 1997 and 1998.
- When Valentino Rossi won the Italian Grand Prix in 2000, Honda posted its 140th 500cc Grand Prix victory, the most in that class of any manufacturer in history.
- Honda also holds the record for the most Grand Prix wins in the 250cc class with 160.
- Since 1949, Honda has won forty-nine Grand Prix manufacturers' world championships, out-performing all its rivals.
- Honda riders have won thirteen of the last nineteen AMA 250 supercross championships.

Italian sensation Valentino Rossi, aboard the final version of the NSR500 and on his way to his first 500cc world crown in 2001. In 2002 Rossi repeated the feat with the new RC2112 990cc V5 four-stroke.

Honda dominated at 250cc level. Here, German Anton Mang tucks his Marlboro-supported NSR250 machine inside Frenchman Jean-Francois Balde aboard a similar but Rothmans-backed NSR.

2 'Oyaji' – Soichiro Honda

Soichiro Honda was an extraordinary man. Not only was he the father of the modern motorcycle as it stands today, he created a motor vehicle industry when it simply should not have been possible. The time when most motoring pioneers created their companies had been at the turn of the twentieth century, when Ford, Peugeot and Daimler were created – not in the post-war era. Shipbuilding magnate, Henry J. Kaiser, had tried to break into the auto business in 1947 – but despite his wealth and experience had lasted only a decade. In short, that territory was already taken. By then, transportation was a mature industry, and its giants wanted no new competitors. By mid-century, one man could no longer create such a manufacturing empire – but Honda was no ordinary man.

It's easy to say Honda's circumstances were different: post-war Japan needed transportation, and Honda seized the moment. Yet so did many others, only to fail. Like the USA, Japan already had its established automotive and motorcycling giants, but Honda somehow made himself their equal.

Soichiro Honda is often painted as a results-oriented pragmatist, not given to suffering fools gladly – but he was much more than that. At his core he was driven by a dream. He was both a visionary and a down-to-earth engineer.

The eldest son of a blacksmith, Soichiro was born in Komyo, near Hamamatsu in November 1906. The turn of the century was a crucial time for Japan. The country was at the junction of old and new, sweeping from agri-

culture to manufacturing, and though he had no interest in blacksmithing (which to him represented the old), Honda's fascination in all forms of machinery was kindled at his father's small workshop where he helped with bicycle repairs. At the age of eight Soichiro saw his first car and ran after it in wonder.

Machinery made sense to the young Soichiro – but book-learning did not. He lacked the patience to wait to gain the school

Soichiro Honda, aged about eight.

36

Next to engines, Soichiro Honda loved motor racing best. He raced automobiles during the 1930s until he had a serious accident. In the 1950s he visited the Isle of Man TT races and vowed to race there himself. The company has, to a large degree, dominated the event ever since.

diplomas that might help him in the future – instead he plunged headlong into practical work with cars and engines.

Aged sixteen, he left school in 1922 and was awarded an apprenticeship at a motor repair business in Tokyo. In 1928 he returned to Hamamatsu to start a similar business of his own. He did well, became wealthy and indulged in power boating and motor racing. In 1936 he was leading the All-Japan Automobile Speed Championship when he crashed at high speed, sustaining major injuries from which he needed months to recover.

During his convalescence he came up with a plan – to move into manufacturing rather than repair. His first product was to be piston rings since he reckoned there would always be demand for them. So he took out a loan and purchased a small factory. That company was called the Tokai Seiki Heavy Industries

(TSHI). Fifty workers were hired and production started. But the rings proved to be useless as they were far too brittle. To solve the problem, he took them to the professor of metallurgy at the nearby Hamamatsu Institute of Technology who found them to be deficient in silicon.

Until this point in his life, Honda had relied on his strong practical abilities for problem solving. He now realized that he needed more theoretical knowledge for his new venture and so enrolled himself on a two-year course in metallurgy. He never actually received his diploma because of his failure to attend lectures that he did not think worthwhile. But this was typical of Honda's approach to learning. He believed that what was important was the knowledge itself, not the associated bits of paper. His first successful piston rings were manufactured in 1937.

World War II presented further problems. Because most of his skilled workers were enlisted, he could only obtain unskilled women as replacements. So, to get round this, Honda designed and built machinery that produced piston rings automatically whilst being tended by these inexperienced workers. He followed this up with a design for a high-speed planing machine that would automatically form the complex curves of the wooden propeller blades he was making as part of the war effort.

This awareness of both his own abilities and the abilities and needs of others, allied to an innate ambition, characterized Honda's whole life. He knew his own countrymen well enough to lead them, and he sought in others talents he himself did not have. He was certainly no isolated engineering 'nerd', dreaming in private. Honda demanded practical results, and found a way of working to achieve them. He learnt to regard failure as a necessary step towards understanding and ultimate success and he instilled in others the drive to learn and to experiment without the fear of failure.

This was the philosophy that lay behind the company that tried and failed with its revolu-tionary NR500 four-stroke GP racer in the late 1970s and early 80s – and then produced the NSR500 V4 two-stroke which dominated Grand Prix racing for a decade in the 1990s. It was also the philosophy behind the Gold Wing.

Honda's success was soon noticed by others. In 1942, one of his customers, *Toyo Kogyo* (now known as the Toyota Motor Company) bought 40 per cent of TSHI.

But it was not all success. In 1944 the Honda factory was bombed and in January 1945 it was hit by an earthquake. Shortly after the end of World War II Honda sold the remaining 60 per cent to *Toyo Kogyo* and, quite uncharacteristically, decided to take a complete break from work for over a year. He dismissed the idea of returning to the manufacture of piston rings and instead turned his thoughts to other money-making ideas.

The economy and infrastructure of Japan had been badly damaged during the war and there was a great need for simple, basic transport. It had to be economical as fuel was in short supply and therefore rationed. Honda decided he could meet this need and founded the Honda Technical Research Institute in

Though the Honda Motor Company was very much the product of the engineering genius and driving personality of its founder, Soichiro Honda (left), one other man came a close second. Takeo Fujisawa (right), his trusted lieutenant, was the marketing brains.

The 1960s proved to be the making of Honda. Starting the decade by making tentative forays into foreign markets, by the end the company was the world's leading motorcycle producer, winner of multiple world championships and maker of the CB750 Four, the world's first superbike.

October 1946. It was in fact no more than a tiny wooden shed on a bombsite in Hamamatsu containing Honda and ten employees – but Honda had a vision.

Seeing a desperate need all around him in war-scarred Japan for basic, affordable transport, he hit on a scheme. He had been fortunate in obtaining a batch of 500 small petrol engines that had been used to power portable generators for the army. He attached these to bicycles to make them into primitive mopeds and they were a great success, especially as Honda even produced the fuel to run them on. He had bought a pine forest with his father and by distilling an infusion of the tree roots managed to produce turpentine, which had an

enormous advantage over other fuels in that it was not rationed. This was then mixed with petrol to form a low-grade fuel.

After the initial batch had all been used up, Honda continued by making his own engines – basically copies of those he had bought in. The new bike was officially called the Model A and the first example was produced in November 1947.

Honda's experience with his piston-ring business had instilled in him the value of continuous reinvestment in technology. He realized that it was not enough to have a good idea and a willingness to put in the hours – if you made a product no better and no worse than your competitor's, the customer had no reason

Soichiro Honda on the assembly line. He was known affectionately by his workforce as Oyaji *or 'Dad'.*

and applied this approach to everything in his working life. He showed a famous disrespect for status, believing instead that work dignified the workman – thus began the Honda corporate philosophy whereby all workers were known as 'associates' – as they are in the Maryland Gold Wing plant to this day. By the same token, work clothes and cap were deemed equally appropriate for board meetings or shop floor visits. Honda expected to be judged by his actions, not by the cut of his suit, and applied the same standards to his workforce.

Soichiro Honda's unconventional ways also became the personality of his company. He did not subscribe to socially correct theories of management through compromise and consensus decision-making. He did, however, strongly believe in a hands-on approach – he was everywhere in the flesh, checking the progress of R&D projects, visiting production shops, helping workers assemble an engine, injecting his own views, asking questions. Honda's way was to overturn the conventional to seek out ideas so simple that the traditional thinkers had overlooked them. In his view, engineering was not just applied science; it was imagination made real and useful. 'What do you need?' he asked the world. 'We'll make it.'

Honda believed that the high quality which came from a creative combination of design for use and design for manufacturing was all for nothing if it failed to fulfil a specific market need. In other words, a product that can be made in easy steps can be made well, and a product that does its job reliably pleases its users.

The step-through Honda Cub of 1958 was the first international success for the Honda Motor Company, and became the model for all the successes that were to follow. The Cub was also an embodiment of the Honda philosophy: 'Recognize a need, create a unique way to satisfy it, incorporate unusual performance, quality and reliability, then build from an

to prefer yours. But reinvestment in technology offered something different – a way to grow ideas into useful new things that people would want.

While his powered two-wheelers were a great success, Honda did not rest on his laurels. He knew it would take something more to succeed in the turbulent 1950s, and it was during this time that he propagated a stream of innovative designs which were to make the company the world leader in motorcycle engineering within an amazingly short time.

Honda learnt to reach goals by breaking with tradition and being, inwardly at least, a colourful non-conformist, he would happily do so. His novel way of seeing the world owed much to his playful sense of humour. He learnt early that unconventional ideas could work expanding reputation into yet other areas'. A need was recognized, and after trial and error, the trouble-free, easy-to-operate 50cc Cub was created.

In addition to challenging conventional manufacturing methods, he also changed motorcycle and automotive marketing techniques. Most famously, he introduced the advertising slogan 'You Meet the Nicest People on a Honda' to the USA in the 1960s – and within the decade dominated the market.

Honda's refreshingly simple marketing approach targeted the general public with good, clean two-wheeled fun and introduced

millions to motorcycling. And when that entry-level market was saturated, Honda had the vision to see that a similarly trouble-free kind of sports motorcycle could become equally popular, building on the proven reputation of the Cub. As that success spread to many countries, Honda expanded its line, always offering customers a step up to more sophisticated models. Soon after came auto production, and the rest, as they say, is history.

Competition was also a major part of Honda's philosophy. An enthusiastic competitor himself, Soichiro attended the Isle of Man TT Races during his first visit to Europe in 1954 and was in awe of what he saw. On his

In 1968, Soichiro Honda was at the centre of celebrations to mark the production of the company's ten-millionth machine – in fact he rode the bike off the Hamamatsu production line himself.

return to Japan, realizing the great benefits it would bring, he immediately made motorcycle racing success one of the company's prime goals: when his motorcycles won their first Grand Prix road racing titles in 1961, the new company's engineering power was demonstrated to the world. Since then, racing has remained a valued element in Honda's development process. From this continuing research and development, a long succession of technological triumphs have resulted including low-emission engines, variable valve timing, and lean-burn combustion.

All of this success was no accident, no fluke of birth. Soichiro Honda reinvented himself and learnt, often the hard way, how to succeed in the most difficult commercial arena of all. His company became an extension of himself, displaying his qualities and employing his methods. Honda's unconventional personality proved to be an invaluable asset in an era of rapid and unpredictable change, enabling the company, like the man, to make room for itself among less agile giants.

Soichiro Honda was known affectionately to his workforce as *Oyaji* (Dad). This was no blind devotion. Honda succeeded because he encouraged, nurtured and managed others to succeed themselves. He inspired everyone around him to use their imagination and give their best. He was willing to put his trust in young people and give full rein to their creativity.

Believing that people should advance on merit and not through nepotism, Honda refused to put relatives in senior posts, and when he retired in 1973 he put the company in the capable hands of Kiyoshi Kawashima. Soichiro then devoted himself to the Honda Foundation, seeking harmony between technology and the environment. Having fulfilled countless dreams over half a century, he died in 1991 leaving his wife, Sachi, a son, two daughters and a very different world from the one he'd entered eighty-five years before.

3 'King of Kings' – The M1 Project

The M1 was built to find out what was possible –
Soichiro Honda

For a flagship machine that not only heralded a whole new class of motorcycle but then went on to beat off all competitors, successfully reinvent itself over a period of twenty-five years, become a massive sales success and ultimately so definitive of its type (and even within motorcycling as a whole) that it now transcends even the name Honda, it's hard to believe that the Gold Wing was nearly never born at all.

In 1972, three long years before the Gold Wing was finally unveiled, Honda had set up a project team to explore the outer limits of motorcycle design and to develop the concept of a revolutionary long-distance superbike. The project, code-named M1, laid much of the groundwork for the Gold Wing that was to follow.

At that time, the bounds of workable displacement and engine layout were being pushed further back every few years and new designs were continuously being released by a variety of manufacturers in a bid to appeal to a rapidly expanding market. By 1972, Honda's own original superbike, the 1969 CB750, had already been overtaken by Kawasaki's 900cc Z1. Prior to the Z1, Kawasaki had launched its radical, hooligan 500cc, two-stroke three-cylinder H1 in the same year as the CB750 – followed soon after by the even more powerful 750cc H2. Suzuki had followed too, with its own wild two-stroke, the liquid-cooled,

three-cylinder GT750, or 'Kettle' as it became affectionately known. Yamaha, meanwhile, developed its short-lived TRX750 four-stroke twin.

At the same time, however, some other companies were fiercely resisting the temptation to experiment – notably Harley-Davidson and BMW. With BMW slowly evolving its boxer twin – the R75/5 then being the latest incarnation – and Harley-Davidson showing a steadfast loyalty to its 45-degree, pushrod V-twin, these two marques were maintaining a commitment to evolution rather than revolution and were retaining a loyal customer following by doing so.

Soichiro Honda was determined to regain the mantle of the king of superbikes by building a new corporate flagship and in so doing challenge what was currently thought possible. Irked by Kawasaki's Z1 and the continued dominance of BMW and Harley-Davidson in the touring sector, Honda wanted the largest, fastest and best touring machine ever produced. He wanted nothing less than the 'King of Motorcycles'. Of course, the ultimate question was just how big, powerful and wild could a two-wheeled vehicle be and still be a motorcycle?

To address this question, a group of engineers met at the Honda factory at Wako, southern Japan, in the autumn of 1972. Attending were many of the men responsible for some of Honda's most successful designs of the 1960s, including the brilliant Soichiro Irimajiri.

Irimajiri had been the head of the design team responsible for the amazing five- and six-cylinder road racing engines in the mid-1960s and would later give Honda the very successful CX500 V-twin, CBX1000 six-cylinder and revolutionary oval piston NR500 GP racer of 1979. He was to become vice-president of Honda Motorcycle R&D before finally moving up to become chief executive of Honda of America Manufacturing, where the Gold Wing would ultimately be built. In the meantime he became the head of the M1 Project.

What was needed, Irimajiri told his colleagues at a meeting in 1972, was a machine to uphold Honda's corporate pride in the face of new opposition – a machine that would be acclaimed as the world's fastest and best grand tourer.

Despite drawing heavily on existing designs from both the motorcycle and automotive world, the machine the designers eventually produced was unlike anything ever seen before. Although the project was code-named M1, the machine itself was also known as the 'AOK'. Only one version was ever built and though it was finally abandoned it was, in every sense, the father of the Gold Wing that would follow.

What Irimajiri and his team of brilliant young engineers correctly identified was that the largest potential market for their new motorcycle would be in the USA. Accordingly, they began by checking out the local competition to see how it shaped up. Only one rival existed – Harley-Davidson's vast ElectraGlide. Despite still using an ancient air-cooled, 1200cc pushrod V-twin engine, the Glide was large, strong, comfortable and fast enough to carry big Americans over big American distances. What it lacked in sheer speed was compensated for by sheer torque, but the Harley's engineering qualities left plenty of scope for improvement.

That criticism could not be levelled at the other contender on sale in the USA – the

BMW boxer twin. Though only manufactured in small numbers compared to the Japanese, it was built to very high standards and had a very loyal following because of it. Like the Harley, the BMW was a fundamentally simple motorcycle using a straightforward air-cooled twin-cylinder layout that had been refined over several decades. Its main problem was that the vibrations produced by the engine transmitted themselves to the rider in the form of shudders and there was also a significant torque reaction under heavy acceleration and braking due to the shaft drive. The BMW also suffered from a lack of substantial luggage carrying capacity and as American tourers preferred to travel with everything but the kitchen sink, the German twin's gross weight limit was too easily surpassed.

It was with these influences in mind that Irimijari's team began to conceive their new machine. The specification demanded a high gross weight limit that in turn required a wide rear tyre. A powerful, large-capacity engine would be necessary to power all this weight up hills, together with liquid-cooling to keep things quiet and cool and a multi-cylinder configuration so that the power delivery was smooth.

It is also important to realize that the M1 was conceived and executed by engineers – not stylists, marketing types, accountants or even the public. Thus, for the sake of smoothness, the engineers chose six cylinders laid out in a horizontally opposed configuration, similar in concept to a Corvair car engine but unlike anything that had been developed for a motorcycle before. Its displacement was 1470cc, 2cc shy of doubling the CB750's 736cc displacement and larger than even some cars. Other design features inspired by the car included liquid-cooling (air-cooling was the motorcycling convention), single ohc above each cylinder block driven by belts (the Z1 had twin cams) and an alternator that rotated the opposite way to crankshaft direction to reduce lateral torque.

Less radical by motorcycling standards were bore and stroke dimensions of 72 × 60mm (but don't forget the M1 had six cylinders) and a compression ration set at a very mild 8:1. Similarly, just a single two-barrel downdraught carburettor took care of induction. Peak power was 80bhp at 6,700rpm.

That output may not sound much for a full 1500cc engine by modern standards, but at the time it wasn't far behind the then benchmark Kawasaki Z1 – and, remember, the M1 was intended primarily as a touring machine.

Housing that humungous engine was a steel tube double cradle frame with an engine mount layout similar to the CB750. The entire rear end mimicked contemporary BMWs – the gearbox, drive shaft, rear hub, seat and mufflers could almost have come straight off the German machine.

Considering the engine's sheer bulk, the M1's all-up weight was surprisingly low – just 484lb (220kg) and its wheelbase an impressively petite 58.2in (1,480mm). Conversely, tyres were standard fare for the time – a 3.25 × 19 at the front complemented by a 4 × 18 at the rear.

This large displacement had made several things very possible. One was sizzling performance: top speed was reported at around 130mph (209km/h) with a standing quarter-mile time around twelve seconds.

Some within Honda wanted to tune the engine for even more power – at this time, horsepower was still considered the single most important factor in the public's eyes. Furthermore, it was what the initial M1 project goals called for. Others, whose opinion eventually won the day, saw the flat-six as more of grand touring engine, with a nice, fat power band, tons of roll-on torque and silky-smooth power delivery. As the M1's development progressed, the ebb and flow of engineering and corporate politics pulled the machine further

The M1, a liquid-cooled flat-six which blended a BMW-style shaft-drive rear end with a disc-braked CB750-type front and a big automotive-style engine in-between. Note the 'Lion' name on the pannier.

Later early design studies for the forthcoming Gold Wing reveal the influence of the M1. Bodywork and the fact that a four-cylinder engine was now being used in place of the flat-six, much of the M1 remains . . .

This later-still styling sketch is even closer to the M1, mimicking its forebear's slab-side tank and slim tank-seat unit.

in the direction of touring on a grand scale – yet again uncharted territory for motorcycling in general and Honda in particular.

Naturally enough, the engine smoothness was exceptional – as was stability due to the bike's low centre of gravity. But the M1 was not without its faults. The main problem was one of comfort – the length of the engine made a decent riding position almost impossible and it was too much of a stretch to the handlebars.

Even Soichiro Honda himself had reservations. He believed that buyers of the day had a psychological threshold of 750cc and that anything larger would be ill-received. This is backed up by the fact that many of the styling mock-ups and artist's renderings of the time portray 750s: GL750 Four, Gold Wing GX 750 and X-I 750. He also favoured the simplicity of air-cooling.

The upshot of it all was that the M1 project

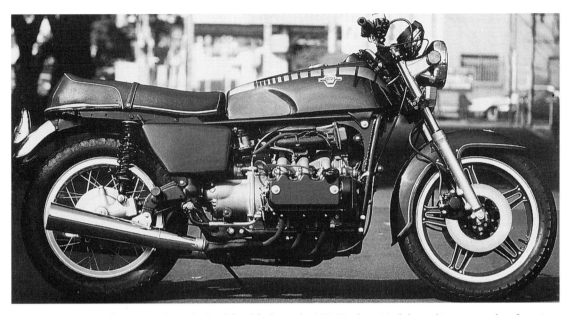

Note the late 1970s-style ComStar front wheel and flared fender on this M1. Honda revisited the machine on a number of occasions when evaluating modifications to successive generation Wings.

was called off – although the 'King of Kings' project continued – and Honda instead reverted to a four-cylinder configuration that was ultimately to become the GL1000.

Of course the influence of the M1 remained. In 1972 the idea of a liquid-cooled, flat-four, shaft-drive motorcycle was nothing less than revolutionary and the GL1000 could never have taken to the road just three years later without the M1 paving its way.

With more then twenty years of Gold Wings burned deep into our consciousness, the M1 still looks familiar today, like a stripped down GL1500. And, of course, most ironically of all, the Gold Wing itself did, in 1988, return to the flat-six layout pioneered by the M1. In fact, during the early stages of GL1500 development, the old M1 was wheeled out, dusted off and its six-cylinder engine was bolted into a GL1200 chassis to test its feasibility.

Not a bad legacy for a motorcycle that never saw the light of day.

4 The Dynasty Begins – The GL1000

Although the M1 of 1972, based on a flat-six engine with a displacement of 1470cc, was a failure, Honda decided to continue the King of Kings project and set up a new design team to head the process, now code-named Project 371. Toshio Nozue took over from Irimajiri as project leader and set about creating an innovative, world-beating grand tourer to be known as the 'Gold Wing' after the company's emblem.

Like Irimajiri, Nozue came to the project with impressive credentials. Although he was essentially a frame designer, already to his

credit were the CB750 Four and two-stroke 250cc Elsinore off-roader.

The revived King of Kings project also included a few new parameters. The engine was to be the new machine's heart and so had to be both larger than contemporary super-bikes such as the Kawasaki Z1, BMW R80S and Moto Guzzi V7, and more powerful than the prevailing king tourer, the Harley-Davidson FLH1200 ElectraGlide. As the M1's 1470cc capacity had been deemed too large, Honda decided that a flat-four was a more practical solution. The team eventually settled

This left-hand side view of the bike emphasizes the first Wing's chunky but compact styling. The large side panels cover the unusual underseat fuel tank – the dummy above the engine was used as a storage compartment and to hold the electrics.

Styling sketches drawn early in the Wing's development show how quickly the basic form of the machine had been decided.

on a displacement of 999cc with an oversquare bore × stroke of 72 × 61.4mm and many of the features inherited from the M1.

Like before, the flat-four layout necessitated liquid cooling, but as there was no other liquid-cooled motorcycle around in 1973, the Honda engineers studied the best automotive designs instead. Having learnt from the M1 experience, they wanted the engine to be as compact and smooth as possible, so rather than looking at previous motorcycle designs they again looked to the automotive industry, studying the work of Porsche, BMW and Chevrolet.

Many other ideas engineered into this new touring machine were also unprecedented in modern motorcycling, for example dual disc brakes, a 'hidden' fuel tank and mid-range power delivery with the emphasis on torque.

Other radical ideas were experimented with but rejected: fuel injection was dropped because of concerns over side-of-the-road repair difficulties. Automatic transmission was scrapped due to excessive size and weight (it was later trialled again with the CB750A of 1978). An electro-hydraulic centre-stand was deemed too heavy, while anti-lock brakes were simply not practical with the existing technology. These ideas would have to wait for the later Gold Wing derivatives.

The irony is that although the first GL1000 seemed revolutionary in 1975, a prime example of what we know today as 'thinking outside of the box', individually, none of the Wing's features were actually very new.

Liquid cooling had previously featured on the 1908 Scott (unbeknown to Honda who

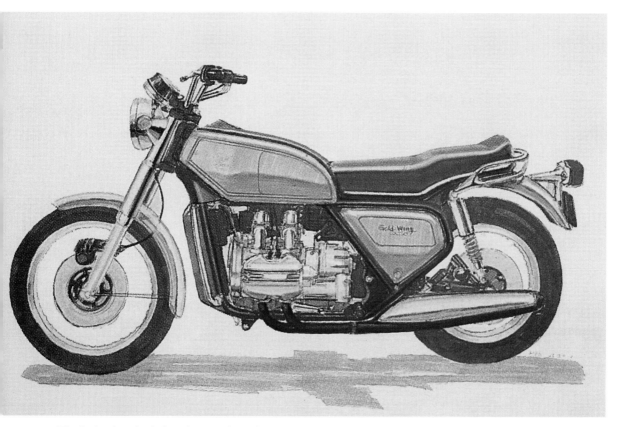

This final styling sketch shows how true the production model remained – even the badging on the side panels, the tank and chrome-shielded silencers are identical.

thought it was producing the world's first liquid-cooled motorcycle); toothed rubber cambelts had been seen on the slightly earlier Moto Morini 3.5, while both BMW and Moto Guzzi had long featured shaft drive.

However, the Wing was unique in combining several features from the motorcycle and automotive worlds and successfully blending them together in one machine. What really set the Gold Wing apart was its size; its performance, which rivalled anything on the market; its unparalleled long-distance ability; plus automotive-like service intervals and reliability. The Gold Wing revolutionized motorcycle thinking and almost single-handedly created the modern age of motorcycle touring.

At its heart was the engine: essentially two 180-degree parallel twins set beside each other with the right-side cylinders staggered forward. The automotive part of the mix was that the cylinders were cast in one piece with the crankshaft halves. When the left-hand crankcase was removed, the pistons exited from the bottom of the cylinders. Removal of the right cylinders required the unbolting of the con-rods: the pistons and rods then came out through the tops of the cylinders.

The clutch and gearbox could have come straight off the CB750 motorcycle. The wet multiplate clutch comprised seven friction plates (from the CB450 twin) and eight plain ones, but as only one of the two steel plates actually transmitted power, clutch failure was common on early models. The entire gearbox and selector mechanism even included identical ratios, although few parts were actually interchangeable. Continuing the family connection were the clutch springs, these having being seen on the earlier CB72 twin.

As with the M1, there was a single ohc on each cylinder bank driven by toothed rubber belts. Although relatively new to motorcycles at the time, such belts were common in cars and by that time Honda was also a successful car manufacturer. It's no coincidence that the Gold Wing's cam timing belts were virtually identical to those on its Honda Civic car.

Four 32mm Keihin constant vacuum carburettors were used on the original machine, helping to give a peak power output of 80bhp – enough in 1975 to put the first Gold Wing truly into superbike territory.

The hemispherical cylinder heads had generously sized valves and ports, indicating that the engine was in a moderately high state of tune. The inlet valves were 1.45in (37mm) with 1.26in (32mm) exhaust valves – fairly large for cylinders of 250cc each. In order to fit these valves, they were offset on opposite sides of the combustion chamber centreline, just like the CB750. Also like the CB750 was the valve and camshaft layout. The camshafts were in two sections and supported by aluminium bearings, these sharing the high-pressure oil feed from the rockers. The camshaft timing offered reasonably long duration for a touring bike.

The pistons provided a compression ratio of 9.2:1 and while the claimed maximum power figure was only 80bhp, this was undoubtedly pessimistic – the straight-line performance of the first Gold Wing placed it truly in superbike territory.

Although the carburation set-up, using four 1.25in (32mm) Keihin constant vacuum carburettors, was essentially conventional motorcycle, the position they occupied, particularly with the airbox above, led to another clever deviation from conventional practice – in order to maintain a low centre of gravity, the actual fuel tank was positioned beneath the seat, between the frame tubes. However, that brought the fuel level so low that a car-style fuel pump was then required to provide a constant fuel supply, driven from the right camshaft.

Meanwhile, drive to the five-speed gearbox was via a conventional motorcycle multi-plate clutch rather than a BMW automotive style single plate affair.

Another feature, which undoubtedly added to the Wing's appeal as a touring bike, was the use of shaft drive. Such systems were previously the preserve of European manufacturers such as BMW and Moto Guzzi, but the incorporation of the drive shaft through the centre of the right side of the swingarm was a first for Japanese manufacturers.

The centre section of the dummy tank was hinged and could be raised, and the side folded down to allow access to the machine's electrical components and a small storage space.

As such, it took Honda longer to develop than many other components. As this was long before the days of computer-aided design, stress analysis testing necessarily included brutally abusing the prototype's drive train by shifting into first gear while rolling at 30mph (50km/h) in neutral. This abnormal torture prompted violent rear wheel hopping but also provided Honda's engineers with vital information on the strength of the Wing's drive shaft. As the Gold Wing was a vitally important model for the company – arguably its most important since the CB750 Four – the prototype underwent a much longer testing period than Honda's usual eight months, with

development riders punishing the machine for a full year at Honda's Tochigi test facility.

Another time-honoured feature that Honda perfected for its flagship was a spring-loaded shock absorber incorporated into the drive shaft – its origins going back to the primary drive shock absorbers in pre-war British singles. The swingarm itself pivoted on needle bearings, a much more effective system than Honda's usual plastic bushes.

All of these features indicated Honda's intention to create a machine of exceptional quality. However, while the drive shaft itself may have been functional, simple practical features such as easy rear wheel removal to repair a puncture or change a tyre were overlooked. As a result, rear wheel removal required the lowering of the entire exhaust system. However, other basic maintenance tasks were indeed easier than on most other bikes. As the cylinder heads were easily accessible, valve adjustment by screw and locknut was relatively straightforward. Routine maintenance also called for periodic timing belt adjustment, but no more so than on a comparable car.

But perhaps the biggest advance for motorcycles with an in-line crankshaft was the secondary use of the AC generator as a counter-rotating flywheel to cancel out the severe torque reaction of the crankshaft. It had become apparent to Honda that this had kept many prospective buyers away from BMW and it was hoped that by tackling the problem in this way the Gold Wing would tempt a whole new generation of touring motorcyclists.

As with the engine, there was little truly revolutionary about the Gold Wing's chassis – but some of the features were innovative for touring motorcycles. In 1975 a rear disc brake was very much a novelty. Furthermore, the Wing's rear disc was much larger and more powerful than those on the front. Made from stainless steel, it was a full 11.6in (295mm) in diameter and was grasped by a dual-opposed piston brake caliper. The discs at the front, meanwhile, were 'only' 10.7in (273mm) and had single floating piston calipers.

Another, truly innovative feature of the front brake set-up (that will be barely noticed today) was the siting of the twin calipers behind the fork legs rather than in front. All disc-braked machines at that time featured forward-mounted calipers, but, as the Gold Wing was to prove, it made more sense to mount the calipers at the back to get the weight closer to the steering centreline and thereby reduce steering inertia. An additional benefit was that the front wheel could be more easily removed for tyre changes.

The practice of employing a larger rear disc brake was to set the touring style for years to come – even conservative BMW eventually succumbed – while by the late 1970s virtually all production machines used rear-mounted front brake calipers.

In an era when skinny front telescopic forks predominated, Honda took the step of increasing the fork leg diameter from 1.37in (35mm) of the CB750 to 1.45in (37mm) for the Gold Wing. And to further increase rigidity there were also four clamping bolts underneath each fork leg for the axle. At the rear were rather limp twin shock absorbers, adjustable only for spring preload.

The frame, however, was a conventional tubular steel duplex full cradle type with an unremarkable 28-degree head angle while the wheels were conventional wire-spoked loops. However, one quality touch was the use of lightweight aluminium-alloy rims instead of chromed pressed-steel to minimize unsprung weight – although it seems trivial, given the Wing's massive overall bulk. Unfortunately, these were to prove one of the Wing's weak points as they were not suited to the machine's power and weight, and after just three years were replaced by Comstars in 1978.

Completing the Gold Wing's impressive specification was a fat (for its time) 4.50H ×

17A Bridgestone Superspeed 21-R2 rear tyre which had been specially developed for the 584lb (265kg) machine. (There was a wild suggestion at the time that during 1975 Honda had spent a massive £500,000 in developing the rear tyre, although Toshio Nozue always denied this.) In truth, its size was inspired by that of its great rival, the Harley-Davidson ElectraGlide – but unlike the Harley, the Gold Wing came with a more conventional 19in front wheel, this time wearing a 3.50H × 19 Bridgestone Superspeed 21-F2.

Finally, the bike's overall physical size was cleverly kept to a minimum – even the wheel-base was a fairly moderate 60.6in (1,540mm) – significant considering the problems engineers had faced with the M1.

Equipment and attention to detail also set the original Gold Wing apart from the masses. There was a 'beeping' indicator alarm; the starter motor cut out if the clutch was not engaged when the machine was in gear. And the choke lever, unlike other bikes where it was usually hidden awkwardly under the tank, was positioned conveniently on the instrument console.

The final version was conservatively styled with simple, understated logos and minimal pinstriping. The colours were Candy Antares Red or Candy Blue Green.

In fact, so good was the final prototype that only three small features were later changed for the first production GL1000K0 machine. Self-cancelling indicators were ditched, there was a different radiator cap and a warning sticker was added to the tank.

So, after two years of give and take, trial and error and countless hours of breakthrough engineering, the first GL1000s landed in the world's motorcycle shows and fairs and, in due course, dealer showrooms. And 'landed' just might be the right word.

In October 1974, the first official model, the Honda GL1000K0 Gold Wing, was introduced to the world's press and public during

In comparison with the rest of the machine, the instrumentation of the GL1000 was fairly conventional, with twin dials for speedometer and tachometer with a strip of warning lights between. The 'tank'-mounted fuel gauge would be deleted in later years.

the IFMA (*Internationalen Fahrrad- und Motorrad-Ausstellung*) in Cologne, Germany.

Although there had been gossip circulating for some time prior to its official release, Honda had successfully kept the Gold Wing's actual configuration and capacity top secret. The rumour-mill had suggested a larger, but conventional CB750-type engine – or even a

V6. But all the speculation was comprehensively laid to rest on that fresh autumn morning in Germany. It was the most important new Honda motorcycle since the CB750 five years before, and Honda had undeniably created a showstopper. The Gold Wing was a motorcycle that was impossible to ignore and one about which everyone, not just motorcyclists, had an opinion – and not all of it was good.

The problem was that the first 1975 Gold Wing was the most un-motorcycle looking motorcycle in modern history and sceptics were not impressed – some even suggesting that it looked like a two-wheeled car.

It is very easy to forget that these first examples were born naked – they had none of the accessories they went on to accrue and become inextricably associated with in later years. So when the first GL1000K0 entered the world in 1975 it was a pure, uncluttered roadster – and it was also one of the fastest superbikes money could buy.

Although aimed at riders the world over, the Gold Wing's main market was always intended to be the USA where blistering acceleration sold motorcycles. In fact 'big' sold motorcycles. Period (as they say).

So what Honda had produced was a shaft-drive tourer that could also blow most of the superbike opposition away at the drag strip. US magazine *Cycle* got its hands on a Gold Wing in early 1975 and put it through the standing quarter-mile at just 12.92 seconds. At that time, only two stock production motorcycles had posted quicker times – the Z1 Kawasaki and its already deleted stablemate, the 750cc H1 two-stroke triple. The new GL1000 also proved a premier league machine in terms of outright top speed. Most early road tests reported a best of just over 120mph (193km/h).

But there was a body of opinion that perhaps Honda had gone too far. The only larger machine at that time was Harley's ageing

The first GL1000 Gold Wing was officially unveiled at the IFMA Cologne Motor Show in October 1974 and was the centrepiece of Honda's stand.

Although shaft drive was nothing new, the Wing was the first big Japanese bike to be so equipped and accounted for much of the machine's long development period.

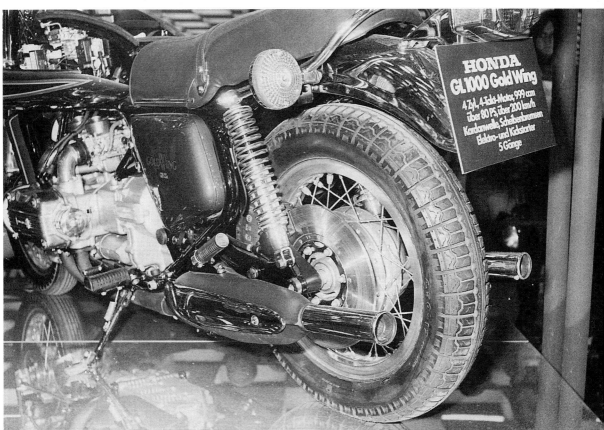

The first production GL1000. Almost a lightweight compared to what was to follow in later years, but in 1975 a revolutionary behemoth.

1975 GL1000

The original GL1000 Gold Wing, powered by a 999cc engine. The dummy fuel tank contains electrical components and storage space. Spoked aluminium rims are standard. Note the black exhaust system with chrome heat shields and tailpipes. Only 5,000 were sold during the first year.

Engine type:	ohc opposed-four, liquid-cooled
Bore × stroke:	72 × 61.4mm
Displacement:	999cc
Carburation:	1.25in (32mm) CV
Starting system:	Electric plus kick
Transmission:	Five-speed
Final drive:	Shaft
Chassis:	Steel, dual shock
Front brake:	Dual disc, single-piston caliper
Rear brake:	Single disc, single-piston caliper
Wheelbase:	60.6in (1,540mm)
Seat height:	31.9in (810mm)
Fuel capacity:	5gal (22.7ltr)
Dry weight:	584lb (265kg)
Colours:	Candy Red, Candy Blue
Prices:	USA (east) $2,881, (west) $2,889

ElectraGlide. The Wing's massive weight of 645lb (293kg) alone was enough to put off many customers and led to the GL's 'Lead Wing' nickname.

What many had failed to notice was that Honda had positioned the Wing's weight as low as possible by moving the fuel tank under the seat. So what appeared to be a conventional petrol tank between the seat and handlebars was in fact a dummy. Lifting the top flap revealed not 20-odd litres of fuel but a small storage compartment. Underneath a plastic tray was the air cleaner and fuel filler cap and then, after loosening a couple of fasteners, the side of the 'tank' could be pivoted down too. On the right-hand side was the radiator's coolant header tank, along with an emergency kickstart lever. Underneath the left-hand cover were the electrical components, all systematically laid out and all easily accessible. Many thought the compartment too small to be of much practical use although the fuel gauge which was incorporated into the top of the 'tank' was widely appreciated – it was also the first time that such a feature had appeared on a production motorcycle.

The other thing that set the Gold Wing's engine apart from its contemporaries was its astonishing quietness. Undoubtedly the water jackets soaked up a fair amount of the noise, and the use of toothed belts was a quieter option than the more usual steel chains. However, most of the credit must go to the bike's massive silencers. The welded-together steel exhaust system was painted black with a chrome shield and tail pipe.

But there was no getting away from the fact that the Wing's engine was also heavy. With carburettors but without engine oil, the flat-four weighed a massive 212lb (96kg), making the engine unit alone heavier than a complete 1975 CB125S2. Despite this bulk, however, the unit was surprisingly compact and almost cube shaped, its dimensions being roughly 25.9in (660mm) wide, 20.9in (533mm) long and 19.9in (508mm) high.

At $2,900, the GL1000 had indeed set a new touring standard. The beefy frame would gladly accommodate aftermarket accessories such as bags and a fairing. The drive shaft eliminated the ritual of perpetual chain lubing with all the associated mess, and the whopping engine could whisk a pair of riders and all their luggage along endless miles of blacktop with ease and a reliability that allayed much of the fear of striking out for a long-haul motorcycle adventure.

But its true potential would not be fully realized right away. Honda had hoped to re-create the wildfire success of the CB750 Four which had sold in tens of thousands during the first year of production, and were looking to sales of 60,000 Wings worldwide during the first twelve months. The actual sales of just 5,000 units were a massive disappointment. Much of the blame for this very discouraging state of affairs was laid at the door of an advertising campaign, which promoted the Wing as 'the ultimate all-rounder' instead of focusing on its core merits as a fast grand tourer. But even with that corrected, it took years for the

big Wing to gain the acceptance and popularity it deserved.

Significantly, 4,000 of those first-year sales were in the Gold Wing's prime target market of the USA. So what about Europe? There, motorcycling habits were totally different. Enthusiasts rode their bikes 'flat-out' wherever it was possible – and sometimes where it was not. Europeans loved the unlimited speed possible on the German autobahns and the challenging mountain switchbacks that criss-cross the Alps. And in this context the GL1000 was a bizarre irrelevance. Its frame was not built for this type of riding, its weight compromised its handling and its engine was conceived for smooth cruising rather than aggressive blasting.

Sweden was one of the few European countries where the Gold Wing found early success with nearly 600 machines registered in its first year. To Swedes, the Gold Wing became a good alternative to the more traditional BMWs and Guzzis that had led its touring market up to 1975.

For 1976 the Wing was essentially unchanged save for the introduction of a new colour scheme – Sulphur Yellow – and the important addition of an external grease nipple to the drive shaft. Other minor modifications were the addition of two helmet holders, the change in colour of the clock faces to light green, the inclusion of a wiper on the oil sight window and a carburettor link guard.

In addition to the standard GL1000K1, there was also a new model, the GL1000LTD. Available only in custom Candy Brown, this bike featured gold anodized wheel rims laced by gold-coloured spokes, gold logos and gold pinstriping plus a chrome-plated radiator shield. It also received a dual-contoured seat, a slightly flared front mudguard, a special toolkit in a leather-effect bag, a gold-stamped owner's manual, and a leather key fob. The LTD was available only in the USA at the premium price of $3,295 and only 2,000 were imported, making it something of a rarity today.

There was, however, a sea change in the way the Wing was perceived. A new advertising campaign paid dividends and the USA suddenly woke up to the merits of Honda's new flagship.

At that time, the USA was the biggest motorcycling country in the world, and therefore a very important market for Honda. Slowly, Americans were coming round to the Gold Wing's combination of high power, fast mileage and 'easy riding'. Furthermore, the Wing was starting to change Americans' riding habits. At a time when few motorcycles left the factory with the reliability or the legs to cross the USA in comfort, the original Gold Wing delivered both. It had suddenly become fashionable to use motorcycles on long-distance journeys – and what motorcycle could possibly fit the bill better than a Wing? A new era of motorcycling had begun.

More than 20,000 Wings were sold in 1976, its second year, and the GL1000 was suddenly set on its way to becoming the founding father of a whole dynasty of Wings that have become

The GL1000LTD was only available in the USA and no more than 2,000 were built.

1976 GL1000 Standard & LTD

A new model marks the Gold Wing's second year. The GL1000 LTD features gold striping, special LTD sidecover badges, a chromed radiator shroud and screen, a quilted contoured seat, gold wheels and spokes, a slightly flared front fender, a gold-stamped owner's manual and leather key case. Only 2,000 were imported into the USA.

Engine type:	ohc opposed-four, liquid-cooled
Bore × stroke:	72 × 61.4mm
Displacement:	999cc
Carburation:	1.25in (32mm) CV
Starting system:	Electric plus kick
Transmission:	Five-speed
Final drive:	Shaft
Chassis:	Steel, dual shock
Front brake:	Dual disc, single-piston caliper
Rear brake:	Single disc, single-piston caliper
Wheelbase:	60.8in (1,544mm)
Seat height:	31.9in (810mm)
Fuel capacity:	5gal (22.7ltr)
Dry weight:	584lb (265kg)
Colours:	Standard: Candy Red, Solid Yellow LTD: Candy Brown
Prices:	Standard: USA (east) $2,960, (west) $2,942 LTD: $3,295

The 1977 GL1000K2 featured a recontoured seat, higher handlebars and chrome covers for the exhaust pipe headers, although the black finish on the exhausts remained.

one of the most popular motorcycles of all time.

Meanwhile, the Gold Wing's British importer, Honda (UK) Ltd, also produced its own limited edition version, similar to the LTD, although on a smaller scale. To promote a prestigious image for the slow-selling machine, British accessories manufacturer Rickman was commissioned to produce fifty-two Gold Wing Executives, one for each week of the year. Setting it apart from the regular Gold Wing was a black paint finish, a frame-mounted Rickman fairing, engine protection bars and a rack plus US-made Lester cast-alloy wheels.

There was a new project team leader for 1977. Masaru Shirakura had previously been involved in the development of some of Honda's smaller models, particularly in the 125–175cc range.

The GL1000K2 model saw a few more detail modifications in 1977, notably to improve comfort and reduce noise. There was a new

1977 GL1000

Only the standard model is available this year. Honda begins to incorporate small but important refinements based on customer requests as the Gold Wing continues to grow in popularity. Chrome heat shields on the header pipes are now standard, as is a higher, recountered handlebar, redesigned neoprene grips and a new dual-contoured seat.

Engine type:	ohc opposed-four, liquid-cooled
Bore × stroke:	72 × 61.4mm
Displacement:	999cc
Carburation:	1.25in (32mm) CV
Starting system:	Electric plus kick
Transmission:	Five-speed
Final drive:	Shaft
Chassis:	Steel, dual shock
Front brake:	Dual disc, single-piston caliper
Rear brake:	Single disc, single-piston caliper
Wheelbase:	60.8in (1,544mm)
Seat height:	31.9in (810mm)
Fuel capacity:	5gal (22.7ltr)
Dry weight:	595lb (270kg)
Colours:	Black, Red
Price:	$2,938

dual-contoured seat, recontoured handlebars that were 2.6in (67mm) higher than before with neoprene bar grips instead of the previous plastic type. The steering head now featured taper roller bearings and the exhaust header pipes had chrome covers to hide the black painted finish. A modification to the clutch now saw both steel plates carry the power, although this still did not solve the clutch problems. To reduce noise further, the engine casings were slightly thicker than before. Two new colours, Circus Blue and Black joined the continuing red scheme. The tank featured more pinstriping while the clock faces reverted to plain black.

The first fundamental changes came in 1978 with the introduction of the GL1000K3 (or KZ in the USA). Another new project leader, Masahiro Senbu, set out to address previous criticisms that had included disappointing low- and mid-range power, poor comfort levels and inadequate wet-weather braking. Thus there were major changes to the wheels, instruments, seat and engine. There were also significant changes to the styling.

Slightly smaller 1.2in (31mm) Keihin CV-type carburettors combined with shorter valve timing and more ignition advance. Despite retaining fairly tall gearing, engine response was significantly improved although claimed peak power was slightly reduced to 78bhp.

Another engine modification was the new exhaust system. Now fully chromed, with two small silencers replacing the giant U-shaped silencer/balance pipe of previous models, not only did the new system make a better sound but it also improved the bike's looks and allowed easier access to the clutch. Finally, the kickstart was at last deleted.

Comfort was improved by an assortment of suspension modifications. Fork travel was increased by 1in (25mm), damping was improved with new damping rods that contained more and bigger holes. Static friction was reduced with chamfers cut into the bottom of the fork tubes to channel oil between the

---

1978 GL1000

A new instrument panel fitted to the centre pod with fuel, voltage and coolant temperature gauges helps distinguish the GL in its fourth year. Honda also fitted smaller carburettors and FVQ shock absorbers with two-stage damping. The exhaust system has been redesigned and chromed, the rear turn signals are now mounted on the fender, the kickstarter has been deleted and the troublesome wire wheels replaced with bolted-up, maintenance-free ComStars.

Engine type:	ohc opposed-four, liquid-cooled
Bore × stroke:	72 × 61.4mm
Displacement:	999cc
Carburation:	1.2in (31mm) CV
Starting system:	Electric
Transmission:	Five-speed
Final drive:	Shaft
Chassis:	Steel, dual shock
Front brake:	Dual disc, single-piston caliper
Rear brake:	Single disc, single-piston caliper
Wheelbase:	60.8in (1,544mm)
Seat height:	31.9in (810mm)
Fuel capacity:	5gal (22.7ltr)
Dry weight:	601lb (273kg)
Colours:	Blue, Maroon, Black
Price:	$3,198

---

tubes and sliders. At the rear, new FVQ shock absorbers with two-stage damping were fitted.

Complaints about the wet-weather braking led the US Department of Transportation to investigate the Gold Wing during 1977. Surprisingly, it wasn't the front brake performance but that of the rear disc that was at fault. This led to the recall of all Gold Wings built before 1978 and the fitting of new grooved brake pads, and new discs and brake calipers were fitted to the 1978 model. The discs were the same as those fitted to the CB750F2, and were not only thinner and lighter than before but were also claimed to improve brake efficiency in wet conditions.

The GL1000K3 incorporated major modifications including ComStar pressed aluminium wheels instead of spokes; chromed exhausts; new tank, instruments, seat and side panels plus a host of engine changes designed to improve throttle response, albeit at the slight loss of top-end power.

Hand in hand with the new brakes came Honda's new, patented ComStar wheels in place of the previously troublesome wires. While other manufacturers at the time were moving towards more rigid cast-aluminium hoops, Honda had decided to buck this trend by going for a wheel with built-in flex. The ComStar was made up of an aluminium rim bolted to pressed-aluminium spokes. Unfortunately it was soon discovered that the aluminium spokes were not sufficiently strong to cope with the weight of the Gold Wing, so special versions with steel spokes soon replaced them. Rim and tyre sizes, meanwhile, remained unchanged.

Other modifications to the 1978 bike included a new instrument console. Not only were the main dials now black, but there was also an additional instrument panel built into the top of the fuel tank. This included water

temperature and fuel gauges and a voltmeter. There were also twin air horns, redesigned centre and side-stands and the rear indicators were repositioned on to the rear mudguard to make fitting of throw-over panniers easier. To round it all off, three new colours were introduced: Black, Candy Limited Maroon and Candy Grandeur Blue.

The result of all these changes saw the Wing's dry weight increase further to 601lb (273kg) and there was a slight drop in performance. *Cycle* magazine recorded a standing quarter-mile of just 13.38 seconds at 98.9mph (159.1km/h) on the new bike while its top speed had now dropped below the important 120mph (193km/h) figure.

Because of rapid advances in motorcycle technology, machines from several manufacturers were now ahead of the Gold Wing, simply because they were designed later.

The 1979 GL1000K4, the last of the 1000s, featured detail changes only — rectangular turn signals, a brake fluid master cylinder, black anodized control levers, and a new quartz halogen headlamp.

There was no getting away from it: after three years, the Gold Wing was beginning to suffer in comparison with some of the newer Japanese touring machines, particularly Yamaha's shaft-drive XS1100. The Yamaha was more comfortable, faster, lighter and had better handling. It also had greater load-carrying capacity.

Honda decided that although big changes were needed, they would have to wait until 1980. In the meantime, another new project leader, Ryo Nashimoto, headed the team for the 1979 GL1000K4. For that year the one-piece brake discs also returned, to a slightly revised design, but otherwise the K4 was much as before. Only detail changes were made. These included new rectangular indicators and a brake fluid master cylinder, black anodized control levers and a new twin-bulb tail-light with CBX-style ribbing on the lens.

More than ever, the Gold Wing was need of a make over. In a comparison test of six

1979 GL1000

The GL1000 reaches the peak of its development and is the last Gold Wing to be powered by a 999cc engine. Changes are few and minor: rectangular turn signals replace the previous round ones, control levers change from silver to black and a twin-bulb tail-light with a CBX-type ribbed lens replaces the single-bulb unit.

Engine type:	ohc opposed-four, liquid-cooled
Bore × stroke:	72 × 61.4mm
Displacement:	999cc
Carburation:	1.2in (31mm) CV
Starting system:	Electric
Transmission:	Five-speed
Final drive:	Shaft
Chassis:	Steel, dual shock
Front brake:	Dual disc, single-piston caliper
Rear brake:	Single disc, single-piston caliper
Wheelbase:	60.8in (1,544mm)
Seat height:	31.9in (810mm)
Fuel capacity:	5gal (22.7ltr)
Dry weight:	604lb (274kg)
Colours:	Candy Burgundy, Candy Blue, Black
Price:	$3,698

touring motorcycles that appeared in the US magazine *Motorcyclist* in June 1979, the Gold Wing came out last and was criticized particularly for poor ride comfort, handling and throttle response, as well as being excessively heavy with a peaky power delivery. Honda wasn't used to coming last.

Other factors were at play too: with more than 80 per cent of Gold Wing production now being exported to the USA, it made sense to build a production plant there. Although Honda had been building overseas plants for more than twenty-five years, the move to the USA in the 1970s was risky.

To most consumers, quality was Honda's strongest selling point, and building in the USA could jeopardize this hard-earned reputation – not just for the Gold Wing, but for all Honda products for decades to come. Nevertheless, Honda forged ahead, and on September 10 1979, the first Honda of America Manufacturing (HAM) plant began production in MMP, Ohio.

As for the bike itself, changes were due. . . .

First Press Reviews

In short, some loved it, some didn't. Naturally enough, the most appreciative tests appeared in US magazines. *Motorcyclist* praised 'Honda's ultimate touring master-piece, as the 750 Four that preceded it, will take off on a trip all its own, pioneering a sophisticated concept yet untouched, but soon to be pursued by those destined to follow the leader'.

Cycle first spotted the Wing at a dealer convention in Las Vegas and assumed it to be '. . . a soft, posh and mildly-tuned straight-line tourer'. However, a rapid standing quarter-mile time of 12.92 seconds with a terminal speed of over 104mph (167km/h) soon changed their minds. These speeds were fast for 1975 and all-important to superbike buyers of the era. In the April 1975 issue, *Cycle* enthused:

We don't know how much the GL1000 is going to cost, but however much it turns out to be, it'll be a bargain in terms of utter engine smoothness and quietness, in terms of quality of engineering and new-wave thinking that has gone in to it, in terms of surprisingly agile handling performance and shattering stopping and accelerating performance . . . Here is a tourer, unblurred and brilliantly focussed for those who want nothing to intrude on their feeling of the road and who want to intrude on no-one else as they enjoy it.

On the downside, *Cycle* found that the Wing didn't ride too well over the expansion joints common on LA freeways and that its riding position was too cramped for taller riders. But generally it rated the new Wing very highly, pointing out its excellent reliability which meant that 'all you had to do apart from stopping for gas was to enjoy the trip'.

Motorcycle News, the huge British weekly newspaper, also praised the new Gold Wing, calling it, 'A superb example of Japanese engineering, the biggest and heaviest Honda ever made is a complete breakaway from Honda's previous designs'.

By 1977 the K2 version had acquired a more comfortable seat, taper roller bearings in the steering head and a grease nipple on the shaft-drive housing to make lubrication an easier task – and the plaudits were even greater.

Peter Rae was generally impressed when he tested the K2 version for *Motorcyclist Illustrated* in 1977.

This smooth transition of combustion power into forward motion had made my journey one of the least tiring in my experience. The almost total absence of noise above 50mph also contributed to my comfort, as the water jacketing keeps mechanical sound down to a clicking from the tappets which is soon lost in the breeze. The exhaust too is well silenced, yet emits an authoritative growl when accelerating hard from standstill. Sitting there with only the wind for accompaniment, my ears free from mechanical assault, body enjoying the complete lack of vibration and my senses revelling in the engine's responsiveness, perhaps you will begin to understand why I just wanted to keep on riding.

But of course there was also *Bike*, and Assistant Editor Bill Haylock's near-legendary review from its January 1976 issue. His words best speak for themselves.

When is a motorcycle not a motorcycle? No, that's not a clue for any facetious answers – I'm getting seriously worried at the direction the development of Japanese bikes is taking.

OK, we owe Mr Honda a lot for past services. He and his competitors have done wonders for small cube bikes and have made us realize that big roadburners don't have to shake or leak oil. But I have an uneasy feeling that, as far as big bikes are concerned, the Japs are starting to go over the top. They're trying to turn bikers into socially acceptable two-wheeled motorists.

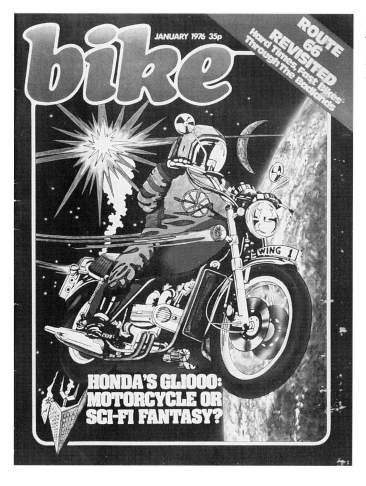

Although press reviews in the USA were generally favourable, Honda hadn't counted on the scepticism of some European motorcycling publications. The UK magazine Bike, *in particular, was unimpressed.*

When Honda's Gold Wing became more than just a well-engineered rumour, Honda's publicity machine rumbled into action like a squadron of Chieftain tanks, hoping to conquer the prestige bike market with battle cries like: 'Quite simply the most advanced motorcycle ever made'; 'Acclaimed as the most significant and major achievement in the motorcycle industry for many years'; 'The Ultimate. . .'. Powerful stuff, even to the experienced connoisseurs of public relations bull. Just about everyone did what was required, and obediently gazed in wonder, instead of asking the question 'The Ultimate what?' No-one looked too closely at the brash claims which, in actual fact, don't stand too much scrutiny. The flat-four motor is nothing new to motorcycles, nor is water-cooling, nor is shaft-drive, nor is the dummy tank, nor is the rear disc brake. One of the biggest, fastest, most complex and impressive motorcycles ever made the Gold Wing may be, but the most advanced. . . ?

In truth the Gold Wing is a very conventional motorcycle. It is remarkable not so much for technical innovation, as for the change of course it represents, away from traditional motorcycle technology and into line with contemporary automobile technology. It also reflects Honda's avowed policy of making the motorcycle more socially acceptable and safer, even if it also makes them more boring.

Honda had been anticipating a much more complimentary piece. In fact, the full review caused such offence that a lengthy withdrawal of its advertising and test machinery from *Bike* followed and the magazine was banned from Honda's press fleet. Perhaps some of Haylock's prophetic words were pitched too close to the truth for comfort.

5 Bigger and Better – The GL1100

The *Cycle World* test that placed the Gold Wing a dismal last in a group test of tourers was the final nail in the coffin for the GL1000. So, after five years at 999cc and with only token development, 1980 saw the first major reinterpretation and re-design of the Wing. And, while on face value alone it seemed as if the new GL1100 was merely a big-bore job, the truth was that in virtually every respect this was an all-new motorcycle.

The competition had already been catching up – Yamaha launched its shaft-drive XS1100 in 1978, and in 1979 Kawasaki supplemented its KZ1000 Four with a new behemoth, the monstrous, liquid-cooled, six-cylinder, shaft-drive Z1300 – and although the Z13 was far from perfect, there was a new boss on the block. It was time for the Wing to move onwards and upwards. While it was obvious that the big Honda needed more cubes and a

The first major evolution of the Gold Wing came with the introduction of the larger GL1100 in 1980.

The new Wing was unveiled in Europe at the Paris Motorcycle Show in September 1979. Although the conservative, evolutionary design was never likely to cause the shockwaves of the original model five years earlier, much of it, in fact, was new.

restyle, Honda's engineers also took the opportunity to address the shortcomings of the earlier machine.

But there was an additional goal. The old GL1000 wasn't to be replaced by a single bike – there would now be two versions available. The unfaired, standard GL1100 would be joined by a full-fairing and luggage-equipped stablemate, the new GL1100 Interstate. The factory (or 'turn-key') full-dress tourer was about to be born.

Both were to feature new 1085cc engines with electronic ignitions (banishing the previous version's points); the chassis would boast air-assisted suspension, a longer wheelbase, new reversed black ComStar wheels, an adjustable seat and bigger tyres. The Interstate, meanwhile, would set new standards for touring comfort and quality with its full fairing, hard panniers and trunk – not to mention the optional stereo.

Again there was a new man leading the project: Shuji Tanaka. His brief was to respond to the criticisms that had been laid at the Wing's door since its launch in 1975. Foremost of these concerned its seat and suspension. However, it was also considered vital to deliver more potency from the flat-four powerplant and to improve the bike's luggage-carrying ability.

Tanaka's background had been mostly in chassis design. He had originally learnt his trade with the (by then defunct) motorcycle manufacturer Tohatsu before joining Honda

way back in 1961. Since that time he had been significantly involved in some of Honda's most important projects, ranging from the C90 Cub all the way up to the massive CBX1000 Six. He was to remain in charge of Gold Wing development for five years.

Tanaka's first concern, naturally enough in view of the new XS1100 and Z1300, was the Wing's engine. To cope with the extra weight of the planned fairings and accessories and also to hit back at the competition, engine capac-

1980 GL1100 Standard & Interstate

The introduction of the second-generation GL sees the standard model joined by the first turn-key tourer – the Interstate. Both are powered by a new 1085cc engine with electronic ignition (no more points). Maximum power is 81bhp at 7,500rpm, maximum torque 66.5lb ft at 5,500rpm. The chassis boasts air suspension with a single-inlet equalizer system at each end, black reversed ComStar wheels, an adjustable seat and bigger tyres. The Interstate sets new standards for touring with its full fairing, saddlebags, trunk and optional stereo.

Engine type:	ohc opposed-four, liquid-cooled
Bore × stroke:	75 × 61.4mm
Displacement:	1085cc
Carburation:	1.1in (30mm) CV
Starting system:	Electric
Transmission:	Five-speed
Final drive:	Shaft
Chassis:	Steel, dual shock
Front brake:	Dual disc, single-piston caliper
Rear brake:	Single disc, single-piston caliper
Wheelbase:	63.2in (1,605mm)
Seat height:	31in (795mm)
Fuel capacity:	4.4gal (20ltr)
Dry weight:	Standard: 586lb (266kg)
	Interstate: 672lb (305kg)
Colours:	Candy Burgundy, Black
Prices:	Standard: $3,798
	Interstate: $4,898

The GL1100's chassis was significantly reworked, including inverted ComStar wheels and uprated suspension.

ity was upped by 10 per cent from the previous 999cc to 1085cc through the use of bigger pistons which took the diameter of each cylinder up to 2.9in (75mm). Compression remained at 9.2:1.

But there were a great many other changes. There had been reports of a small number of crankshaft breakages, particularly in Europe where the bikes tended to be ridden harder and more aggressively. So the new bike's crankshaft was made considerably stronger: main bearing journals were increased to 1.6in (43mm), and the con-rod journals widened to 1.8in (46mm). Complementing the stronger crank came a 0.23in (6mm) wider Hy-Vo primary drive chain with an accompanying set of tensioners.

In view of the clutch problems the earlier engine had suffered from, the new GL1100 was given a completely new clutch with a cast-aluminium basket in place of the previous model's steel version. The clutch plates themselves were 0.27in (7mm) larger than before and there was a revised clutch release mechanism along similar lines to that of the CBX1000 Six. This no longer used the earlier bike's 'scrolling' device with ball and ramp but instead relied on a simpler cam and cast lever. Finally, finishing off the new 1100's internal strengthening was an increase in the output shaft diameter to 1.1in (28mm).

The most significant improvement at the top end of the engine was the addition of another set of new camshafts. These had the effect that, while exhaust valve lift was unchanged at 0.33in (8.5mm), the inlet valve lift was increased a touch to 0.34in (8.8mm). While delivering longer duration cam timing, the usual side-effect is narrower powerbands – not the sort of attribute desired of the Gold Wing. So Honda's engineers countered this by employing smaller carburettors, replacing the previous machine's 1.2in (31mm) Keihins with four new aluminium-bodied Keihin 1.1in (30mm) CV items. The smaller diame-

ters aided low-speed running while responsiveness throughout the rev range was improved by the use of a new accelerator pump for each of the four carburettors.

Finally, the time-honoured mechanical contact breaker points were replaced with electronic ignition. A simple vacuum advance mechanism, similar to that used in the automotive world, was also fitted to marry the degree of ignition advance according to the engine load.

Setting the new GL1100 off were newly designed rocker boxes and all-new secondary reduction and gearbox ratios. The final drive unit itself was now the lighter, more compact unit from the CX500 but with a heavier, sealed U-joint. Overall gearing was slightly lower to improve acceleration.

All of these changes, combined with a 10 per cent increase in the power output to produce 81bhp at 7,500rpm and much stronger mid-range urge. *Cycle* magazine managed a standing start quarter-mile time of 12.47 seconds at 107.39mph (172.79km/h) during its test in January 1980, which meant that the new bike was a whole second faster than its predecessor. Peak torque was now 66.5lb ft @ 5,500rpm. But this improvement in performance was solely down to the new powerplant – although 13lb (5.8kg) less than before, the new GL1100 tipped the scales at 637lb (288kg) wet.

As the new ignition system was mounted at the rear of the engine, the frame had to be made slightly longer than before. The swingarm was longer too, and both combined to give the bike a massive 63.2in (1,605mm) wheelbase. To ensure the new machine was as stable and solid as possible, there was larger gusseting of the frame around the cylinder head, double pinch bolts strengthened the bottom yoke and the steering geometry was set at a very lazy 29.2 degrees of rake with 5.3in (134mm) of trail.

As well as being longer, the new frame was

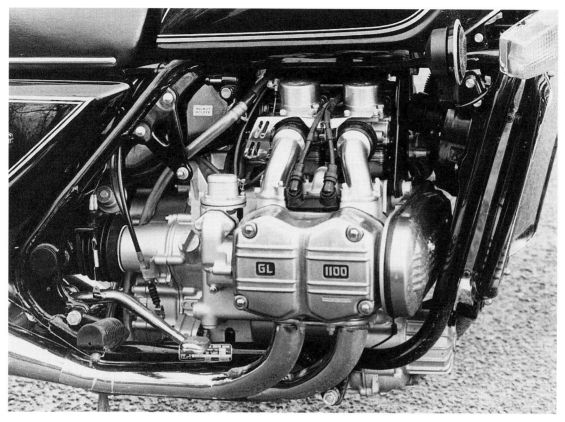

The new GL1100's displacement was in large part a response to competition such as the Yamaha shaft-drive XS1100 launched a year earlier.

also slightly wider and lower to accommodate both a larger fuel tank and provide a lower seat. The result was a seat height of 31.9in (810mm) and a much roomier riding position. The new, bigger Wing was more stable too, with the disconcerting high-speed weave characteristic of the K2 and K3 now a thing of the past.

In view of all this it was no surprise that the bike received a new suspension package too. Honda resisted the prevailing trend towards longer travel suspension and instead refined a short-travel suspension set up with the use of air-springing. Although still using coil springs with a twin-rate spring stacked on top of a single-rate one, most of the support was actually provided by air pressure.

The two fork legs were linked to a single valve on top of the right tube and, with infinite adjustment available between 14 and 21psi, there was a significant improvement over the forks of the previous GL1000. In addition, the diameter of the front fork tubes was increased to 1.5in (39mm) and special low-friction Syntallic bushings made from lead, bronze and Teflon were used inside the legs. These overcame the problem of static friction common in earlier Wings (which were fitted with all-metal bushings).

Air featured in the rear suspension too with the twin shocks also linked to air chambers. Here, the recommended pressure ranged from 29 to 42psi, and if pressure fell below 28psi a red warning light housed in the tachometer blinked at the rider to stay below 50mph (80km/h).

But of course it wasn't just the Wing's engine, frame and suspension that had come in for an overhaul from Tanaka's team. The 1100 also received a new set of reversed ComStar wheels with black spokes and turned-out edges. The front rim size was widened to 2.15in (54.6mm) and it now wore a 110/90-19 tyre on the front with a 130/90-17 at the rear. Completing the new Wing's upgraded specification were the brakes – solid twin 10.8in (276mm) discs again with single-piston brake calipers and a single 11.6in (296mm) item at the rear.

The Wing's riding position and equipment levels were also updated. As most Wings ended up being fitted with aftermarket fairings (around 80 per cent, according to Honda's own research), the new bike's handlebars were re-designed with this in mind. They were huge –

A new quilted and stepped, deeply padded seat provided more touring comfort than ever before while the riding position was canted back slightly and the handlebars raised.

Inspired by the success of sales of aftermarket fairings to Gold Wing owners, in 1980 Honda decided to launch its first faired Gold Wing – the Interstate. This is the OK version without panniers or top box.

33.1in (843mm) wide and extended far back. The dummy fuel-tank doors of the previous bike were discarded and instead all serviceable items could now be reached via a two-piece lid in the top. The redesigned dummy tank lost the three gauges that had featured since the K3 model but which had always proved a hindrance to the fitting of a tank bag. Instead, the fuel and temperature gauges were now placed on top of the instrument console with the voltmeter being discarded altogether.

Rider and passenger comfort was improved with a new stepped seat, which was adjustable by 1.5in (40mm) front and rear. Honda's research had revealed that the previous bike's

seat had been one of the items customers had most commonly replaced with aftermarket items – as was the front mudguard which was now a more deeply valanced type.

Surprisingly, despite all these changes and additions, the new Wing was actually lighter than its forebear with a dry weight of 586lb (266kg). On closer inspection it becomes clear that much of this was down to the use of lighter materials such as plastic instead of steel for the mudguards, side panels, dummy fuel tank and seat base.

Other changes included a new exhaust system which no longer featured the rust-prone balance box of previous bikes in front of the rear wheel; an increase in the fuel tank's capacity to 4.4gal (20ltr); an up-rated 300W, three-phase alternator; and an additional power point for use with accessories. The gross vehicle weight rating was increased to 1,105lb (502kg).

The sum total of all these changes was a machine that was superior in almost every respect to its predecessor. In May 1980, soon after its launch, *Cycle World* magazine ran the new Wing against its closest competitors in a group test. The result? After being so soundly beaten only a year earlier, the new 1100 was once again the class leader ahead of the BMW R100RT, Harley-Davidson FLT-80, Kawasaki KZ1000, Suzuki GS850 and Yamaha XS1100.

And that was just the standard machine. The Interstate was something else altogether.

The Interstate

Although the aftermarket accessory industry had been happily supplying touring equipment for the Gold Wing since its launch in 1975, by 1979 Honda had finally realized the potential profit in supplying official equipment. So, after lengthy consultation with the Gold Wing Riders Association in the USA, Honda produced the GL1100I Interstate (initially called the GL1100DX or De Luxe in Europe) – and it was the bike that many touring riders believed Honda should have produced in the first place.

Honda intended that the Interstate should be the ultimate luxury touring motorcycle, equipped with the highest quality accessories available. Because these accessories would be specifically designed for the Wing, rather than being variants of universal accessories, and would be factory fitted, Honda knew it could provide the Interstate with an integrated look that aftermarket versions sometimes lacked.

The Interstate was fitted with the following extras as standard: full touring fairing, a rack, hard panniers and top box plus engine and pannier guards. In Britain the detachable top box and panniers were options available at extra cost. All body parts were made of injection-moulded plastic, colour-matched to the

The US Interstate came fully loaded, however.

The Interstate was so successful that it not only effectively killed off the aftermarket industry for Gold Wing fairings, it also led to the discontinuation of the naked model.

bike. The fairing came with two inner pockets, one of which was lockable. Furthermore, the left fairing pocket had a provision for an optional radio/stereo/intercom system, which included speakers. An additional instrument console, fitted inside the fairing, could hold four extra instruments and Honda naturally made available a voltmeter, air temperature gauge, altimeter and a clock for the purpose.

The Interstate's extras were of the highest quality. Scratch-resistant Lexan was used for the screen rather than the more common Plexiglass used by most aftermarket manufacturers and the windshield height could be adjusted by up to 1in (25mm). An even taller screen was available as a further option.

Though the panniers were fixed, they offered a full 36ltr of storage space and included a lightweight travel bag. The top box, which was removable, also incorporated an upholstered passenger backrest. The inte-grated look was finished off by setting the indicators into the leading edges of the fairing and lower corners of the panniers.

Although not in the slightest respect cheap, the Interstate was an immediate success in the marketplace. The first Interstate's $4,898 sticker price was $1,100 more than the base GL1100 and optional audio gear could easily add another $1,000 on top of that. But despite some scepticism from the British press, the Interstate found acceptance worldwide. The Wing had already acquired something of a cult status in Europe and the Interstate (or De Luxe) built on that appeal. In fact it was so successful that Honda had plans to cease production of the unfaired standard Wing until it received a deluge of protests from the major US fairing manufacturers. Instead, the standard GL continued in production until 1984.

The Interstate's fairing cocooned the rider so successfully that there was little sensation of

The GL1100 Aspencade was the most luxurious touring motorcycle the world had ever seen.

1981 GL1100 Standard & Interstate

Distinguished by new orange and gold pinstripes, both models boast redesigned instruments with improved night-time illumination. The Interstate also features a new adjustable, scratch-resistant windshield. Honda introduces saddlebag liners this year.

Engine type:	ohc opposed-four, liquid-cooled		Rear brake:	Single disc, single-piston caliper
Bore × stroke:	75 × 61.4mm		Wheelbase:	63in (1,605mm)
Displacement:	1085cc		Seat height:	31in (795mm)
Carburation:	1.1in (30mm) CV		Fuel capacity:	4.4gal (20ltr)
Starting system:	Electric		Dry weight:	Standard: 586lb (266kg)
Transmission:	Five-speed			Interstate: 672lb (305kg)
Final drive:	Shaft		Colours:	Candy Burgundy, Metallic Blue Black
Chassis:	Steel, dual shock		Prices:	Standard: $4,098
Front brake:	Dual disc, single-piston caliper			Interstate: $5,298

speed when riding the machine. The engine's quietness also had something to do with its uncannily tranquil forward progress. Only taller riders felt a little buffeting of their helmets by turbulent air passing over the screen.

Highway stability was also assured due to Honda's carefully designed steering, frame geometry and weight distribution. A 6lb (2.7kg) iron weight between the bike's front fork tubes added mass to the steering assembly, making it less prone to weaving at speed. The downside was that more care was required at trundling speeds as there was extra weight to contend with.

In 1981, the standard and Interstate model GL1100s continued to set the pace for turn-key touring bikes. Distinguished by new orange and gold pinstripes, improvements for the second year of production included a new seat, which was subtly recontoured and lowered yet again. It was now also possible to slide the seat fore and aft by 1.57in (40mm) using a finger-controlled latch. The rear shocks were uprated to improve the ride when fully loaded and the instrument console was redesigned with a tinted shield to cover the warning lights and to improve night-time illumination.

In 1982, the basic GL1100 continued alongside the Interstate and there was again a raft of improvements to both bikes. The front wheel diameter was reduced to 18in, the rear to 16in with the rim width increased accordingly to 2.5in (63mm) at the front and 3in (76mm) at the rear. This was to allow the use of larger tyres – a 120/80 H18 at the front and a 140/90 H16 at the rear – which enabled the gross vehicle weight limit to be increased slightly. These new Dunlop Qualifiers also helped to increase rear-tyre life, which had long been a criticism of previous Wings. To accommodate the larger, fatter rear tyre, the swingarm was widened slightly. The bike's gearbox was revised because of the new wheel and tyre sizes – third, fourth and fifth gears all became slightly higher; and from the CB900

came new slotted front discs and twin-piston front brake calipers.

Other changes included self-cancelling turn indicators (this was the first time they had been fitted since being discarded from the original prototype Wing in 1974) and the extra power socket was uprated to 10 amps to provide more power for the many lights, radios and accessories that riders were adding. In response to complaints from owners, the Interstate's engine protector bars were shortened so they no longer banged the riders' shins so readily. Finally, the panniers were made more water-tight and new air-cushioned passenger footrests were fitted.

The Aspencade

The introduction in 1982 of the third Gold Wing model, the super-luxurious Aspencade, was almost as significant as the introduction of the Interstate had been two years earlier. With the Aspencade (the name was inspired by a Gold Wing rally held at Aspen, Colorado) Honda set out to redefine motorcycle comfort and convenience, and the bike that they came up with was so luxurious that even the Interstate looked poorly equipped.

The basic engine and running gear were unchanged, although the Aspencade received vented, cast stainless-steel discs similar to those on the CBX1000. However, it was the features and levels of equipment that set it apart.

At the heart of these was a signal-seeking (or self-tuning) Clarion Type II AM/FM stereo radio with a remote handlebar station selector, a mute button, a digital dashboard readout and a clock. And if all that wasn't enough, there was the option of an auto-reverse cassette player, four-channel CB radio with handlebar selector, talk switch and intercom.

In 1982 there was no other touring motorcycle like it and the added luxuries and prestige cost only $250 more than the mid-level Interstate, now retailing for $5,448.

1982 GL1100 Standard, Interstate & Aspencade

Honda adds a third model to the GL line, the luxurious Aspencade. The Interstate model offers options such as a new Type II stereo, a 40-channel CB transceiver and an on-board air compressor, but all of these items are standard on the Aspencade. Other standard items include twin-piston brake calipers, wider tyres, storage pouches in the passenger backrest, two-tone paint and seat, a removable trunk, saddlebag liners for ease of unpacking, extra-wide footboards and armrests for the passenger and special-edition Aspencade badges. Furthermore, the instrument panel is now partly digital. This model was only obtainable in the USA. Until 1984 both versions of the GL1100 were available.

Engine type:	ohc opposed-four, liquid-cooled	Fuel capacity:	4.4gal (20ltr)
Bore × stroke:	75 × 61.4mm	Dry weight:	Standard: 595lb (270kg)
Displacement:	1085cc		Interstate: 679lb (308kg)
Carburation:	1.1in (30mm) CV		Aspencade: 703lb (319kg)
Starting system:	Electric	Colours:	Standard: Wineberry Red, Black,
Transmission:	Five-speed		Metallic Black
Final drive:	Shaft		Interstate: Metallic Black
Chassis:	Steel, dual shock		Aspencade: Metallic Brown two-
Front brake:	Dual disc, twin-piston caliper		tone, Metallic Silver two-tone
Rear brake:	Single disc, twin-piston caliper	Prices:	Standard: $4,248
Wheelbase:	63in (1,605mm)		Interstate: $5,448
Seat height:	31in (795mm)		Aspencade: $5,698

The Aspencade boasted luxury features such as a stereo radio, optional CB and intercom, and an air compressor to adjust the suspension. In 1982 there was nothing else like it.

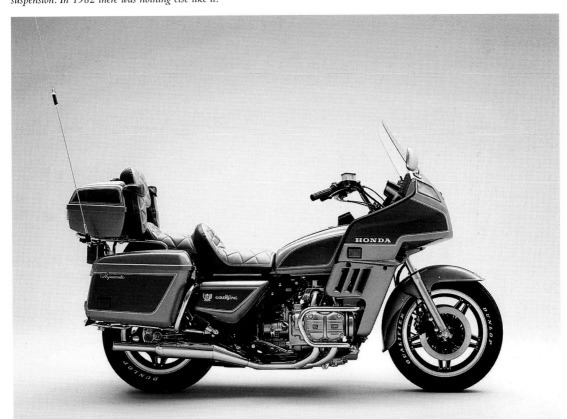

The 1983 Aspencade received improved brakes, suspension and cast alloy wheels.

Another first for the Aspencade was an on-bike air compressor – the air suspension could be adjusted simply by pressing a button, although it could only be adjusted at standstill with the ignition key in the 'P' Park position. The revised air suspension also allowed for a slightly lower seat height of 30.7in (780mm).

Other Aspencade fitments included a larger passenger backrest that came complete with two built-in storage pouches, a vanity mirror in the top box, a map pocket and a higher quality toolkit.

Many of these features, such as the radio, were also offered as options to Interstate buyers. But what undoubtedly set the Aspencade apart were the sumptuous two-tone colour schemes and special edition Aspencade badges.

This was the ultimate two-wheeler for serious travellers. Fingertip control of the standard-fit stereo was a neat refinement for the ever-increasing band of riders who liked to cruise down the highway accompanied by music. The only real downside was yet another increase in weight to 702.3lb (319kg), softening the standing quarter time again to 13.5 seconds.

Honda didn't let up the following year either. In 1983, just as Yamaha and Kawasaki were starting to make inroads into Wing territory with their Venture and Z1300 derivatives, Honda upped the ante yet again.

Most of the changes that year were to the Wing's wheels, brakes and suspension. Most significant of all these was the introduction of Honda's unified braking system (UBS), a kind

1983 GL1100 Standard, Interstate & Aspencade

The last year for the GL1100s finds them fitted with eleven-spoke cast wheels, torque reactive anti-dive control system (TRAC) with an integrated fork brace and a unified braking system. The Interstate has larger, flatter footpegs and adjustable passenger pegs, while the top-of-the-line Aspencade boasts internally vented front brake rotors, a digital LCD instrument panel and a new two-tone seat.

Engine type:	ohc opposed-four, liquid-cooled
Bore × stroke:	75 × 61.4mm
Displacement:	1085cc
Carburation:	1.1in (30mm) CV
Starting system:	Electric
Transmission:	Five-speed
Final drive:	Shaft
Chassis:	Steel, dual shock
Front brake:	Dual disc, twin-piston caliper
Rear brake:	Single disc, twin-piston caliper
Wheelbase:	63in (1,605mm)
Seat height:	30.7in (780mm)
Fuel capacity:	4.4gal (20ltr)
Dry weight:	Standard: 600lb (272kg)
	Interstate: 685lb (311kg)
	Aspencade: 707lb (321kg)
Colours:	Standard and Interstate: Black, Candy Regal Brown
	Aspencade: Candy Wineberry Red two-tone, Metallic Grey two-tone.
Prices:	Standard: $4,298
	Interstate: $5,548
	Aspencade: $5,698

of linked brake system whereby the brake lever on the right handlebar controlled the left front disc while the brake pedal controlled both the rear brake and right front disc. Honda also fitted the bike with its torque reactive anti-dive control system (TRAC) which used brake torque to produce an anti-dive effect.

The Wing's 1.5in (39mm) forks and rear suspension were uprated once again. The spring rates were stiffened all round and the compression damping was increased to reduce the risk of the forks bottoming out.

The rear shocks were modified in concert with this – the spring rate ended up 50 per cent stiffer than before and they could now be run without any air pressure at all if required. Other chassis modifications saw the addition of a VF750S V45 Sabre-style alloy fork brace and new eleven-spoke cast-alloy wheels. (Customer research had indicated a preference for cast-alloy wheels over Honda's unique pressed-alloy ComStars. This led to the introduction of cast-alloy wheels across the entire Wing range, although Honda steadfastly maintained that the ComStars were just as strong.)

And there was still more. The seat height was lowered to 30.7in (780mm) to match that of the 1982 Aspencade. Larger, flatter footpegs and adjustable passenger pegs were introduced to improve comfort and, for the first time, there was a removable section in the rear mudguard to aid access to the rear wheel.

On the Interstate and Aspencade models the engine protection bars now flared outwards to provide more leg room. Changes to the top box and seat also led to increased passenger comfort: the pillion seat was lengthened by 1.2in (30mm) and the rider's backrest was narrowed, also by 1.2in (30mm), to reduce pillion leg splay. In response to criticisms that the pillion backrest was too low, the Wing's entire top box was repositioned 1.2in (30mm) further back and 25mm higher than before.

Not that Honda stopped there – while there was little doubt that the top-of-the-range Aspencade was the most lavishly equipped touring motorcycle money could buy, Honda was not about to rest on its laurels.

By far the most obvious improvement was to the Aspencade's instrument console. In what was a radical update, considering how conservative many motorcyclists are, the

Aspencade received an all-new LCD display panel. Electronic readouts were provided not just for road and engine speed but also for fuel level, engine temperature, suspension pressure and trip distance. The tachometer readout could be switched between a digital display or a graph and there was even a green service light that turned yellow at 8,000 miles (12,875km) and red at 9,000 miles (14,480km). Now there was now no excuse for not having your Gold Wing serviced at the correct time!

All these developments saw the Gold Wing, and particularly the Aspencade, continue to lead the field. With average sales of 25,000 per year, it remained the most popular touring motorcycle in the USA, but the competition was hotting up. In July 1983 *Motorcyclist* magazine voted Yamaha's new 1200cc Venture as the best big tourer. It was time for Honda to retaliate once more.

Made In America – Marysville Motorcycle Plant

As the Gold Wing was always designed primarily for the US market and with over 80 per cent of production eventually ending up in the USA, it was perhaps inevitable that Honda would look at creating a motorcycle production facility there. But when Honda decided in 1977 to build such a plant in Marysville, a small town in America's midwest with a population of just 75,000, it seemed inconceivable to some that such a plan could succeed.

In the 1970s, consumers' attitudes had been hardened by years of disappointment and frustration with American-made products. At the time, 'made in America' was a by-word for poor quality, design and production – best illustrated by General Motors' problems with the Vega, Ford's with the Pinto, and the AMF-built Harley-Davidsons.

Honda, on the other hand, had gained and determinedly nurtured the reputation of the

US workers put the finishing touches to the latest GL1800.

Japanese-manufactured motorcycles for excellent build quality. While Honda's first US plant offered an opportunity to change these perceptions about American quality, there was no doubt that it was a major challenge with significant hurdles to overcome. Furthermore, it simply had to succeed.

Honda's plan was not just for a motorcycle plant – it also wanted to build cars in the USA. But it was decided that a motorcycle plant would be tried first and, if it was successful, the company would proceed with the $250 million auto plant it also planned to build. However, if the Marysville Motorcycle Plant (MMP) failed because of quality problems, Honda's reputation, and its whole future, could have been damaged beyond repair.

But as history shows, the Marysville experiment did everything expected of it. At an initial cost of $50 million, MMP opened on June 10 1979. Only ten bikes were built that day, assembled from imported parts by sixty-four employees. But the overall plant site covered 260,000sq ft (24,150sq m) and would eventually have the capacity to produce 60,000 motorcycles a year. Within just three months it had proved so successful that the opening of the automobile plant was given the green light.

MMP was initially devoted to the production of the Elsinore CR250R off-road machine. Later in 1979 it was joined by the CBX1000, and Gold Wing production started in 1980 with the new GL1100. At last, the Gold Wing had become what it had promised to be all along – a truly American motorcycle.

Initially, most parts were still manufactured in Japan and merely assembled at MMP, but by 1985 fairings and saddlebags were injection-moulded on site and a new engine plant in nearby Anna undertook all the casting, forging, machining and heat-treating processes.

Although built primarily for motorcycles, MMP was designed to allow production flexibility, including the assembly of all-terrain vehicles (ATVs). Thus ten years after the first motorcycle was assembled, the bestselling

Initially, Gold Wing parts were manufactured in Japan and shipped to Marysville for assembly although by 1985 fairings and panniers were injection moulded on the premises. That year also saw the completion of an engine plant in nearby Anna, Ohio. The Marysville plant was completely refitted in January 2000 in order to produce the new GL1800.

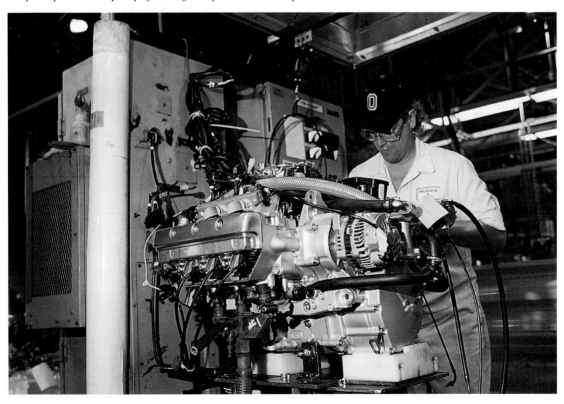

Much of the success of the Maryland plant may be attributed to the application of Japanese corporate philosophy to small-town America. Workers are called 'associates' and dress identically to the management in white overalls.

ATV in the USA, the FourTrax 300, also rolled off the assembly line.

The success of MMP enabled Honda to expand with additional plants throughout the USA: the Marysville Auto Plant (MAP – the first Japanese auto plant in the USA); the Anna Engine Plant (AEP); Honda Engineering North America (EGA); the East Liberty Auto Plant (ELP); Honda Transmission Manufacturing (HTM); Honda Power Equipment (HPE); and Honda of South Carolina (HSC), the company's first exclusive ATV plant.

In January 2000 MMP was completely refitted to enable production of the new GL1800. Two new bays were added to the weld shop to house the sixteen new welding machines needed to handle the GL1800's aluminium frame. The other major change was the removal of engine production from Anna back to MMP. The first GL1800 rolled off the production line on October 10 2000.

Honda attributes the success of its US plants to several factors. First, the physical aspects. Both the 260,000sq ft (24,150sq m) and 330,000sq ft (30,650sq m) HSC plants are far smaller than their counterparts in Japan. The Japanese plants had proved of little use as models, in part because of their much greater production capacity, but also because of their sprawling nature – they had been built and then expanded repeatedly over the years.

The US plants, however, benefited hugely from an injection of Japanese corporate philosophy. Workers were called 'associates' and, while they did not have the lifetime employment benefits enjoyed by their oriental counterparts, they certainly operated in a spirit of cooperation with the managers. All dressed in identical white overalls and were quick to show a commitment to product quality that was often lacking in other US manufacturing plants.

In order to succeed, the US plants needed high levels of efficiency and, in MMP's case, the flexibility to assemble different models. According to Takao Shirokawa, one of the original team members, the plant was designed 'to minimize traffic between adjacent departments, to try to minimize space, and try to maintain efficient logistics inside the plant. We tried to make the most efficient, but small, motorcycle plant. Profitability was the key. So the question was how to minimize the cost of assembly. We tried to pursue efficiency'.

One crucial element of efficiency and quality control at HAM was the use of Honda's own assembly and production machinery. If you were to tour MMP, the HSC ATV plant, or any of Honda's other US facilities, you would see the usual array of Japanese die-cast machines and American tube-benders. But most of the high-tech precision equipment was designed and built by Honda Engineering. Welding equipment used for ATV frames, as well as stamping dies, injection moulds and a range of other machines all bear the Honda Engineering stamp.

Building machines to make machines also provided Honda with a rapid response time. In a competitive market, the ability to react quickly to customer needs gave Honda an invaluable edge. At Honda Engineering – including EGA – engineers were involved at a very early stage in the design process, working closely with those in R&D, thus saving time in creating new jigs, fixtures, stamps and dies. The arrangement also allowed better, more rapid maintenance, as well as *kaizen* – the Japanese word for improvement – of equipment and processes.

Physically, there was little else about MMP and HSC that broke new ground – it was the processes and work practices that made the difference. Take, for example, the sophisticated powder-coat paint process used for FourTrax frames at both MMP and HSC. This efficient, high-quality, low-emissions technology received the Ohio governor's award for

All Gold Wings are given a test run before signing off, although we're not sure if the rider's helmet would pass Ohio highway laws!

The Marysville plant opened on June 10 1979. Only ten machines (built by sixty-four employees) were assembled on that first day. The one-millionth US-built Honda left the production line on 26 July 1996, it was of course a Gold Wing. The first GL1800 was produced on October 10 2000.

outstanding achievement in pollution prevention in 1998.

The attitude the employees brought to their work was also crucial. Before construction began at MMP, Honda officials visited several Midwest manufacturing plants and were impressed to see that the people there possessed a work ethic similar to that of their Japanese counterparts.

As an employer, Honda had a history of treating its 'associates' in ways almost unheard of at other plants. The company believed that a key point in maintaining a high level of quality was to keep their employees involved in and satisfied with their work. For instance, open communication allowed associates to be actively involved in making assembly techniques more efficient. And every associate was treated equally, down to the seemingly minor detail that the workforce shared a single lunchroom, rather than being segregated into labour and management dining areas.

All associates worked to a single pay scale, which facilitated movement from department to department. Such movement allowed cross-training, the development of new skills and a clearer vision of the entire assembly process that has led to many associate-driven improvements over the years.

Honda has also tried to ensure quality by working closely with its suppliers. Initially that was difficult at MMP because of the very low production numbers originally involved – just 150 Gold Wings a day were built there until 1983. Suppliers were unaccustomed to the quality standards Honda demanded, and initially were unwilling to make the necessary investment for such low volumes.

Honda persisted, offering training, advice, and even furnishing equipment – unheard of between client and vendor in the USA at the time and still rare today. And most suppliers appreciated Honda's involvement because it allowed them to improve their own quality, and so expand their businesses. Today, HAM spends $6.4 billion a year on goods and services from some 450 suppliers.

Another important part of ensuring high quality in its US-built ATVs and motorcycles was to monitor quality every step of the way. According to a company spokesman:

> It starts with very high-grade materials, continues with quality suppliers, and then, in a phrase we use, quality in the process. That means we have standards, measurements, repeatable and monitorable, whether it's for a weld or for material specifications for frame material, or the quality of the injection-moulded plastic material – or even how long it stays in the mould. All of those things are very quantifiable for high quality and durability.
>
> But the ultimate standard we apply is customer satisfaction, which has to do with the customers' expectations and how they use the product. If they put a premium on durability and longevity and performance, we have to think up what materials and processes will ensure those things that will satisfy the customer for many years of use.

The construction of the MMP was a huge gamble for Honda – fortunately, one that paid off. The corporate belief that US-based assembly and manufacture could succeed if quality was maintained at every level – people, processes, materials and machinery– turned out to be correct. That commitment ultimately led to the building of seven more facilities in the USA over the next two decades with a total workforce today of over 19,000.

The one-millionth US-built Honda left the MMP production line on 26 July 1996. It was, of course, a Gold Wing.

Honda of America Manufacturing – Facts and Figures

- Honda exports more motorcycles from the USA than any other motorcycle manufacturer.
- It takes more parts to build a Gold Wing than it takes to build a Honda Civic.
- It takes three departments 8.6 hours to build a single Gold Wing.
- More than 2.5 million feet (62,000 metres) of wire is used in a typical year for motorcycle and ATV electrical systems at MMP. That equals 474 miles (762km), or a round-trip from Columbus, Ohio, to Chicago, Illinois.
- For every 160,000 motorcycle and ATV frames produced at MMP (roughly one year's production), 5.9 million feet (1.8 million metres) of frame tubing will be used.
- Since 1979, Honda has used more than 2.8 million pistons in motorcycles and ATVs assembled in US plants.
- Every motorcycle and ATV is tested on a chassis dynamometer before it rolls off the assembly line at MMP and HSC.
- Honda's motorcycles and ATVs are exported to more than forty countries worldwide.
- In a typical year, over 600,000 tyres are used for motorcycles and ATVs made at MMT and HSC.
- HAM relies on more than 353 domestic suppliers.
- HAM produces more than 500,000 automobile and motorcycle engines per year.

The Silver Wing

In the early 1980s, Honda produced a smaller version of the very successful Gold Wing – the GL500 Silver Wing.

Although based on one of the most successful models of the 1970s and 80s – the CX500 – Honda's dream of replicating the Gold Wing formula but in a smaller capacity package did not prove to be a success.

Although the CX had been launched in 1978, primarily targeted at the European market, it did not evolve into the GL500 until 1981. The CX had proved to be a huge success in Europe, despite quickly acquiring the nickname 'the plastic maggot'.

Admittedly it was no beauty – thanks to its odd-looking engine and dubious, bulbous styling – but there was no denying the CX was practical, versatile and reliable, if not exactly exciting. The 496cc, shaft-drive, transversely mounted, liquid-cooled V-twin engine was flexible and easygoing (although it revved too – very oversquare cylinder dimensions of 78 × 52mm allowed a 9,700rpm redline). Long service intervals meant it was reliable, and it was fairly comfortable as well. For those looking for an all-round, workhorse-type middleweight in 1979, the CX500 was the epitome of sensible motorcycling.

Like the Gold Wing before it, Honda's car division and crankcase integral cylinders had influenced the CX. But that was pretty much it when it came to similarities between the two machines. The CX's 80-degree V had four valves per cylinder that were operated by short pushrods in place of the bigger bike's auto-style cambelts.

By 1981, which was the year Honda launched the Silver Wing version, the CX had gained a new chassis, still retaining the engine as a stressed member, but with a single shock Pro-link type rear suspension.

The Silver Wing got the same basic chassis, naturally enough, but as one of the new GL500s was to be a fully loaded Interstate model complete with a fairing and hard luggage, the GL500's engine was uprated too. Two Keihin carburettors now fed the engine, these being closer together and further back than those of the CX500 to provide more mid-range power. The engine was mounted lower than on the CX500 and its wheelbase was longer too at 58.8in (1,495mm).

One unique feature of even the basic Silver Wing was an all-in-one seat and tank unit, complete with built-in rear trunk, which enabled a variety of different seating/luggage arrangements.

However, the basic GL500 was heavy for its capacity at 456lb (207kg) dry. Then there was the even heavier GL500I Interstate, complete with all the full-dresser accoutrements such as a full fairing and panniers on top of that. The Interstate's dry weight was a whopping 507lb (230kg). And all of it had to be pushed around by the 497cc, twin-cylinder engine. All told, the first Silver Wing was a full-sized machine but without full-sized power.

As an essentially overweight, underpowered and expensive touring motorcycle, it's no great surprise that sales did not exactly take off when the bike was launched in the USA in 1981.

With little time to make significant modifications, the two models continued basically unchanged, except for a slight modification to the suspension that improved ground clearance, for 1982. But things still did not get any better.

Then, in 1983, Honda's engineers addressed the one major failing of the Silver Wing. The liquid-cooled V-twin engine was enlarged to 674cc and the GL650 Silver Wing was born.

Other modifications included replacing the unpopular pressed-aluminium ComStar wheels with cast-aluminium items, the frame was strengthened and the spindly 1.37in (35mm) forks were replaced with stronger 1.45in (37mm) air-assisted items.

Undoubtedly, these were all significant improvements but it was a case of too little, too late. The GL650 was still too heavy and after another year of dismal sales the machine was taken out of production and deleted from Honda's range. While the Gold Wing had met all the requirements for success, replicating this with a smaller-engined model was not a winning formula.

Even the name is now no more. In 2001, the Silver Wing moniker was taken over by a new type of machine with very little in common with the Wing – a 600cc scooter, bristling with comforts and luxuries featuring an auto transmission, vast luggage-carrying capacity and all-day 90mph (145km/h) two-up cruising capability. Hang on. Nothing in common with the Gold Wing? Perhaps Honda has finally got it right after all!

Specifications – Silver Wing

	1981 GL500	**GL500 Interstate**
Dimensions		
Overall length:	86.9in (2,207mm)	90.7in (2,305mm)
Overall width:	34.4in (875mm)	34.4in (875mm)
Overall height:	46.4in (1,178mm)	59.2in (1,505mm)
Wheelbase:	58.8in (1,495mm)	58.8in (1,495mm)
Seat height:	31in (788mm)	30.6in (778mm)
Peg height:	12.7in (322mm)	12.4in (315mm)
Ground clearance:	5in (132mm)	5in (127mm)
Dry weight:	456lb (207kg)	507lb (230kg)
Wet weight:	494lb (224kg)	547lb (247kg)
Engine		
Engine type:	Water-cooled, 4-stroke ohv	
Cylinder type:	Opposed V-twin	
Engine weight:	143.3lb (65kg)	
Bore × stroke:	78 × 52mm	
Displacement:	496cc	
Compression:	10.0:1	
Valve train:	Chain-driven camshaft and push rod	
Oil capacity:	0.8gal (3.6ltr) after disassembly	
Oil type:	SAE 10W-40 SE	
Fuel capacity:	3.9gal (17.6ltr)	
Reserve:	0.5gal (2.5ltr)	

	1982 GL500	**GL500 Interstate**
Dimensions		
Overall length:	86.9in (2,207mm)	90.7in (2,305mm)
Overall width:	34.4in (875mm)	34.4in (875mm)
Overall height:	46.4in (1,178mm)	59.2in (1,505mm)
Wheelbase:	58.8in (1,495mm)	58.8in (1,495mm)
Seat height:	31in (788mm)	30.6in (778mm)
Peg height:	12.7in (322mm)	12.4in (315mm)
Ground clearance:	6in (152mm)	5.8in (148mm)
Dry weight:	456lb (207kg)	507lb (230kg)
Wet weight:	494lb (224kg)	547lb (247kg)
Engine		
Engine type:	Water-cooled, 4-stroke ohv	
Cylinder type:	Opposed V-twin	
Engine weight:	143.3lb (65kg)	
Bore × stroke:	78 × 52mm	
Displacement	496cc	
Compression:	10:1	
Valve train:	Chain-driven camshaft and push rod	
Oil capacity:	0.8gal (3.6ltr) after disassembly	
Oil type:	SAE 10W-40 SE	
Fuel capacity:	3.9gal (17.6ltr)	
Reserve:	0.5gal (2.5ltr)	

Specifications – Silver Wing (*cont.*)

	1983 GL650	**GL650 Interstate**
Dimensions		
Overall length:	87.2in (2,215mm)	90.7in (2,305mm)
Overall width:	35in (890mm)	34.8in (885mm)
Overall height:	46.6in (1,184mm)	58.3in (1,480mm)
Wheelbase:	58.8in (1,495mm)	58.8in (1,495mm)
Seat height:	30.5in (775mm)	30.3in (770mm)
Peg height:	12.6in (320mm)	12.4in (315mm)
Ground clearance:	5.9in (150mm)	5.7in (145mm)
Dry weight:	478lb (217kg)	529lb (240kg)
Wet weight:	516lb (234kg)	567lb (257kg)
Engine		
Engine type:	Water-cooled, 4-stroke ohv	
Cylinder type::	Opposed V-twin	
Engine weight:	143.3lb (65kg)	
Bore × stroke:	82.5 × 63mm	
Displacement:	674cc	
Compression:	9.8:1	
Valve train:	Chain-driven camshaft and push rod	
Oil capacity:	0.8gal (3.6ltr) after disassembly	
Oil type:	SAE 10W-40 SE	
Fuel capacity:	3.9gal (17.6ltr)	
Reserve:	0.5gal (2.5ltr)	

6 The Next Generation – The GL1200

Just as had happened three years earlier when Yamaha's XS1100 forced Honda's hand and led directly to the evolution of the GL1100, the emergence of serious competition in the early 1980s forced Honda to rethink its flagship. By 1982, BMW's fully faired R100RT had won a growing number of admirers while 1100cc in-line Fours were also commonplace from rivals Suzuki, Kawasaki and Yamaha, each nibbling away into Gold Wing territory.

But the biggest threat of all came in 1983 when Yamaha launched the XVZ1200 Venture, which soon became regarded as a superbly integrated touring package. Powered by a new V4 engine that was bigger and newer than the Honda flat-four, in pure performance terms the Venture simply left the GL1100 for dead. The upstart Yamaha also handled well and with its swoopy bodywork looked handsome too.

Nor was Yamaha the only challenger. Kawasaki had got in on the act with its Z1300-based Voyager, the largest and most elaborately equipped motorcycle in history. Even Harley-Davidson was showing signs of emerging from its 70s doldrums by re-engineering its perennial pushrod V-twin, and was looking forward to 1985 and the introduction of a new ElectraGlide powered by a new aluminium 1340cc Evolution engine.

Although denied by Honda, there can be little doubt that Yamaha's new Venture and the new Harley-Davidson ElectraGlide Classic had them worried. All this activity led to the design of a completely new Gold Wing for early 1984. The resulting GL1200 was not only a huge improvement over the previous GL1100; it was also designed to maintain a classic link with earlier Gold Wings.

Honda had no wish to alienate loyal Gold Wing aficionados and so deliberately kept the look very familiar. Yet, despite an initial familiarity, everything about the GL1200 was new – engine, frame, suspension, wheels, fairing, luggage, even the seat was new.

Shuji Tanaka again headed the Gold Wing's design team (although this was to be his last year as GL project leader). He quickly found that the main challenge ahead of him was not simply to provide a motorcycle that offered more, but one that maintained the Gold Wing's traditions and did not conflict with the touring culture that now surrounded the machine.

It would have been very easy for Tanaka to take a completely different route. Honda could have discarded the Wing's flat-four engine layout in favour of, for example, a V4 similar to the Venture's. Like Yamaha, Big H had been developing a range of V4-engined machines, such as the VF750 Sabre, and one could have been developed to be at the heart of the new Wing. Indeed, Honda was by then already significantly committed to that engine configuration (today, of all the Japanese factories, Honda is renowned for producing the best V4s, whether in road or racing form). There were even rumours at the time that a vee or even an opposed six could power the new Wing.

However, Honda believed that a flat-four engine layout was more suited to a large touring machine, benefiting from an extremely low centre of gravity for stability and easy manoeuvring. Also, market research indicated that GL owners still wanted a flat-four engine and any new configuration would be seen as a slap in the face. So it was eventually decided that the marque would remain loyal to the flat-four configuration.

At face value, the new GL1200 engine looked to be an evolution of the first GL1000 and indeed bore a striking similarity to the previous 1100cc. But while the basic configuration was the same, almost every component part was new. Only the water and oil pumps were unchanged – and even they were driven at different speeds.

As Yamaha's Venture boasted more power than the GL1100 it was perhaps inevitable that the capacity of the Wing would increase – this growing to 1182cc courtesy of lengthening the stroke from 61.4mm to 66mm and by opening up the bore a touch to 75.5mm. Flatter-topped pistons also reduced the compression ratio slightly to 9:1.

There were similar 'evolutions' throughout the whole bike. In order to increase intake velocity, the inlet valve diameter was reduced by 0.07in (2mm) to 1.4in (36mm) (although the exhaust valve diameter was unchanged at 1.25in/32mm). New cams were introduced, which offered not only increased lift but also more overlap and duration.

Another welcome change to the valve train was the addition of Honda's maintenance-free

This cutaway illustration of the 1984 GL1200 Interstate engine gives some hint of the sophistication and refinement of Honda's proven flat-four.

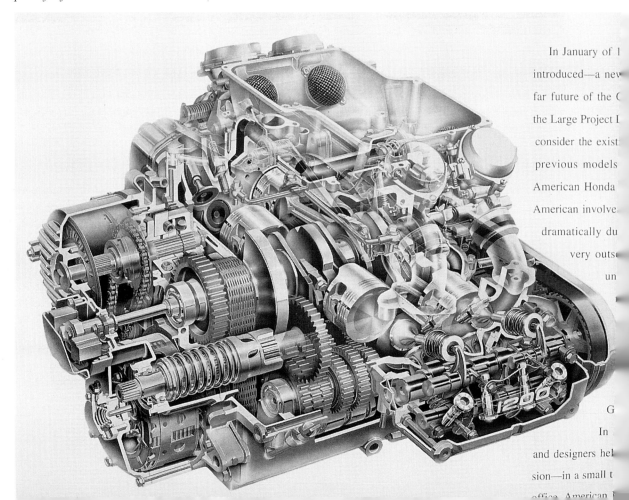

In January of 1
introduced—a new
far future of the (
the Large Project I
consider the exist
previous models
American Honda
American involve
dramatically du
very outse
un

G
In
and designers hel
sion—in a small t

Although superficially similar, the new 1200 engine had little in common with previous models other than the flat-four layout.

hydraulic valve actuation system. This used an eccentric rocker shaft to maintain the correct valve clearance – a system that was by then common to many cars. A hydraulic lifter, pressurized with engine oil, bore on to a flat machined into the rocker shaft while a spring-loaded plunger acted in the opposite direction on another flat. As the camshaft spun and actuated the rocker arm, the eccentric shaft rotated, thus raising or lowering the rocker arm to maintain the correct valve clearance. To save further weight, these adjusters and rockers were fitted into a new magnesium rocker cover.

Maintenance was further eased by the use of a new hydraulic clutch, featuring an additional plate, which automatically took up any wear. (One irony here is that although the emphasis of many of these developments had been to ease maintenance, the new GL1200 continued with an awkward canister-type oil filter which, considering many other Honda motorcycles were already using the spin-on cartridge type, seemed a strange oversight.)

At the bottom end of the engine, the crank was strengthened by increasing the main crankshaft journal diameter to 2in (52mm). A smaller, lighter and more efficient two-row radiator replaced the previous three-row unit, and included, for the first time, an electric fan.

After switching around with the carburettors on the GL1100 there was a return to Keihin 1.25in (32mm) CVs on the GL1200, still fed by a plenum chamber on top of the engine with a cylindrical paper air filter.

To optimize power and economy there was a revised electronic ignition system and, although the internal gearbox ratios were unchanged, the 1200 was bestowed with much taller overall gearing which rendered fifth effectively an overdrive.

The combined effect of all these developments was to raise peak power to 94bhp @ 7,000rpm with an additional 13 per cent

---

1984 GL1200 Standard, Interstate & Aspencade

Honda introduces the new GL1200s. All three models are powered by a new 1182cc engine with hydraulic valve adjustment. Maximum power is 94bhp at 7,000rpm, maximum torque 75lb ft at 5,500rpm. The redesigned chassis sports a 16in front wheel for steering lightness. The Aspencade distinguishes itself from the Interstate with LCD instruments and a special rear lightbar, three-piece removeable soft luggage, and a new Type III audio system with AM/FM radio bands, a cassette player and intercom.

Engine type:	ohc opposed-four, liquid-cooled
Bore × stroke:	75.5 × 66mm
Displacement:	1182cc
Carburation:	1.25in (32mm) CV
Starting system:	Electric
Transmission:	Five-speed
Final drive:	Shaft
Chassis:	Steel, dual shock
Front brake:	Dual disc, twin-piston caliper
Rear brake:	Single disc, twin-piston caliper
Wheelbase:	63in (1,610mm)
Seat height:	30in (780mm)
Fuel capacity:	4.8gal (22ltr)
Dry weight:	Standard: 600lb (272kg)
	Interstate: 700lb (318kg)
	Aspencade: 723lb (328kg)
Colours:	Standard: Wineberry Red, Black
	Interstate: Wineberry Red, Metallic Grey, Pearl Blue
	Aspencade: Burgundy, Pearl Blue, Metallic Beige
Prices:	Standard: $4,795
	Interstate: $6,196
	Aspencade: $7,895

---

increase in torque to 75.2lb ft which together provided vastly improved top gear roll-on performance, despite the taller gearing.

An entirely new, steel tube double-cradle frame chassis was devised to carry the engine. Most significant of all, however, were the new wheels. Smaller in diameter than before and consisting of a nine-spoke, 16in cast-alloy item at the front and a matching 15-incher at the rear, these had the effect of lowering the machine's overall centre of gravity while at the same time providing more responsive steering. While rim widths were unchanged at 2.5in (63.5mm) at the front and 3in (76.2mm) at the rear, a 130-section Dunlop Qualifier was now fitted to the front hoop while a 150-section was worn at the rear. Broader tyres meant that the swingarm had to be widened, while the engine was now angled up by 5 degrees and positioned 2.5in (63mm) further forward in the frame to put more weight over the front wheel.

Things were further improved by moving the steering head back (and lowering it by 1.2in/30mm), which put more weight on to the front wheel, improved the bike's mass centralization and gave more legroom to the rider. The steering rake was also increased slightly, to 30 degrees, although trail was cut a touch to 4.6in (118mm).

The final chassis development, aimed at further improving the motorcycle's handling, was to the suspension. A new, stiffer front telescopic fork arrangement employed 1.6in (41mm) stanchions, still wearing Honda's torque reactive anti-dive control system (TRAC), and there were stiffer springs for the twin rear shocks too.

Just as important to many were the host of improvements to the faired models' bodywork, luggage systems and auxiliary equipment. Visually, the new fairing may have more than echoed its 1100cc forebear, but again it was entirely new. Those on both the Interstate and Aspencade 1200s were completely re-

The new GL1200, here in Interstate guise, was Honda's response to growing competition from the Yamaha Venture and Harley-Davidson ElectraGlide. Superficially it looked very similar to the 1100, yet almost every component was new. Note the angle of the engine in the chassis.

designed with the aid of a wind tunnel to improve aerodynamics and reduce buffeting and wind noise. As a result, the fairing-mounted mirrors, designed to deflect wind from the rider's hands (although UK versions still featured handlebar-mounted mirrors) were integrated into the bodywork, while a taller screen kept the breeze away from rider's head and also reduced buffeting and wind noise.

The bikes' luggage systems were uprated too. Although the topbox was no longer detachable, it was extended and remodelled to provide increased passenger back support. A by-product of this was that the top box luggage capacity increased – by a whopping 50 per cent – enough for it to easily accept what has today become the full-dress standard of two full-face helmets. Each of the panniers was enlarged, this time by 15 per cent.

Yet more carrying capacity could be found in the fairing itself. Each fairing pocket now offered 2ltr of storage space – and this was true of the Aspencade too, as its radio had been repositioned from the left-hand fairing pocket to the centre of the fairing above the handlebar.

Nor was comfort forgotten. There was yet another new seat, containing firmer foam than before, while the seat adjustment lever was now positioned inside the dummy tank rather than under the seat itself.

Then there were those changes metered out solely to Honda's own 'King of Kings' – the Aspencade. Continuing as the top-of-the-range Wing in 1984, the new 1200 Aspencade featured a Hondaline Type III radio (now built by Panasonic instead of Clarion), which was much lighter and more compact than the previous Type II. The stereo system featured a self-seeking AM/FM radio complete with digital display plus four programmable buttons, an auto-reverse tape deck, intercom, manual and automatic muting. There was a handlebar-mounted remote control to enable the rider to retune while on the move (although this was an expensive option on the Interstate) and even an automatic volume control mechanism that compensated for road noise at speed.

The downside was that, despite all its sophistication, the unit's numerous controls

The new 1200's fairings, luggage systems and instrumentation were far more integrated and sophisticated than before.

The new all-digital LCD instrument console was impressive but it did not find favour in all quarters. Note too the growing complexity of the handlebar controls.

made for a massive cluster of switches and buttons on the bike's left-hand handlebar, although admittedly it was much simplified over previous Aspencades.

The Aspencade, alone in the 1984 Gold Wing range, received a revised digital console while the regular GL1200 and Interstate models retained their dual analogue instruments. The bar-graph tachometer from the 1983 Aspencade was ditched in favour of a digital readout only. The LCD readouts continued for the speedometer, tripmeter, gear position indicator, fuel gauge, air suspension pressure gauge and coolant temperature indicator. The only analogue readout, as before, was the milometer.

New footboards and armrests on the Aspencade provided increased passenger comfort and a unique 'signature' light fitted across the rear of the top box left fellow travellers in no doubt as to the exact identity of the machine they were following.

Although the unfaired standard Gold Wing now weighed a reasonably modest 665lb (300kg), the new Aspencade weighed in at a massive 790lb (358kg) when fully fuelled. Yet both machines were far more agile than their predecessors. The new GL1200 steered and handled like a much smaller machine – no mean feat on a bike that still had a wheelbase of 63.4in (1,610mm).

In Aspencade trim, complete with distinctive and luxurious two-tone paint, the Gold Wing was once again truly the king of the road.

There was a new tautness about its ride that transmitted more 'feel' to the rider and thus a greater sense of confidence. The GL1200 had light handling even at walking pace, flicked from side to side with ease and, at speed, maintained a respectable composure through the bends – none of which could have been said about previous Wings.

One of Honda's main aims for the new 1200 – to increase output at low revs – appeared to have been achieved because the new bike felt more tractable. Yet the bigger motor remained the most civilized and quiet unit around – indeed, some owners were tempted to 'blip' the throttle now and again just to make sure the engine had not fallen out! In top gear at 60mph (96km/h), the GL1200 simply purred along at just under 3,000rpm.

Yet despite this, any performance advantage promised by the engine's improved power and torque was wiped out by the increase in weight and taller gearing. Although Honda's engineers had managed to disguise the new machine's weight, the 1200 engine still was not quite as strong as that of Yamaha's Venture. *Cycle* magazine, testing an Aspencade in February 1984, managed a standing start quarter-

The 1975 GL1000. The first Gold Wing, as unveiled to an astonished motorcycling public in the autumn of 1974. Is it a motorcycle? Is it a car? No-one in Europe knew quite what to make of it.

The 1976 GL1000. For its second year changes were few but an additional limited edition model, the GL1000 Limited Edition, was also launched. It was sold only in the US and came only in metallic brown, but also boasted gold anodized wheel rims, gold-coloured spokes, gold emblems and striping, and a chrome-plated radiator shield.

The 1977 GL1000. 1977 saw only subtle modifications to Honda's 'King of the Road'. The seat was re-contoured in an attempt to improve comfort, the handlebars were reshaped and the exhaust header pipes now also received chrome covers to match the silencers.

The 1978 GL1000. The first significant changes came in 1978 with new ComStar wheels, improved suspension, fully chromed exhausts, a raft of engine modifications and new bodywork, too.

The 1979 GL1000. In 1979 there were only detail changes. The indicators were now rectangular rather than round, the headlamp was uprated and there was the usual new choice of colour schemes.

The 1980 GL1100 Interstate. The first 'full dress' version, the Interstate, became available with the new GL1100 Gold Wing in 1980. Apart from a significantly improved engine and chassis, it boasted a factory-fitted touring fairing plus panniers and top box. The full-dress tourer was born.

The 1981 GL1100 Interstate. The only change for 1981 was the introduction of a new seat which was not only recontoured again, but was now also adjustable.

The 1982 GL1100 Aspencade. An even more luxuriously appointed Gold Wing followed in 1982 – the Gold Wing Aspencade. The name was inspired by the name of a Gold Wing rally in Aspen, Colorado.

The 1983 GL1100 Aspencade. More changes: note the new cast alloy wheels replacing the previous pressed aluminium ComStars, and improved brakes.

The 1984 GL1200 Interstate. The third-generation Gold Wing got yet more cubes, a reworked chassis and even more extravagent bodywork. Note how the new engine is angled back in the 1200's frame.

The Limited Edition GL1200LE followed in 1985 and trialled fuel injection and sophisticated digital instrumentation. Although the bike itself wasn't a particular success, features such as these have become fundamental to later Wings.

The 1986 GL1200SE-I. Another limited edition version and another attempt at fuel injection.

The 1987 GL1200 Interstate. The last year for the 1200. By then the naked version was long gone and the full-dresser class firmly established with competition growing from the likes of Yamaha, Kawasaki and Suzuki.

The 1989 GL1500SE. Honda responded to the competition with the all-new, fourth generation GL1500, six cylinder Gold Wing. The opposition had no reply – it was simply astonishing.

The 1991 GL1500SE. Few changes, apart from the inevitable variation in colours, were made for 1991. Few were necessary. The GL1500 has no peers . . .

The 1999 GL1500SE. After ten years at the top the GL1500 was only just starting to show its age, and still has a massive following today.

A big headlamp and lashings of chrome guaranteed the right look for the Valkyrie; hefty 1.7in (45mm) upside-down forks and uprated brakes and chassis ensured excellent handling.

The design group focuses on the mechanical designs. Two sub-groups are then created to produce competing designs.

This front three-quarter view of the new GL1800 displays clearly the Gold Wing lineage. But those twin-spar frame rails and the new 1800cc engine hint at another story.

mile of 13.4 seconds at 89.54mph (144km/h), a speed that was certainly more super-tourer than superbike.

It wasn't perfect in other respects either. Many still found the Wing's fuel gauge as inaccurate and erratic as its forbears; while the jumble of wires and cables running down the left handlebar gave a rather messy look, out of character with the rest of the neatly finished bike.

However, generally it was agreed that the new GL1200 was a vast improvement over the GL1100. It was nowhere near as top heavy as the V4 Yamaha Venture and was much better balanced than Kawasaki's Voyager. The trouble was, the new GL1200 wasn't deemed *hugely* superior to the Yamaha Venture either, although, for the time being, that was enough. While the Venture was close, the Honda Gold Wing remained the benchmark for years to come, the standard by which all other touring motorcycles were judged.

1984 was the final year of the basic, unfaired Gold Wing. Buyers had found the factory-fitted fairing and luggage of the Interstate and Aspencade models so well designed that they tended to go straight for those, even though the unfaired bike, retailing at under $4,500, was considerably cheaper. The withdrawal of the 'bargain-priced' Wing passed with little acknowledgement and virtually no protest – the Interstate, retailing at around $6,200 was now the cheapest model.

The following year, 1985, was to be another significant year for the Gold Wing, although in more subtle ways. In a year of many new beginnings, leadership of the Gold Wing's development team passed from Shuji Tanaka to Hideaki Nebu.

Following the success of Marysville Motorcycle Plant (MMP), Honda built a plant in nearby Anna, Ohio, to manufacture Gold Wing engines. Just as MMP's success paved the way for Honda's auto manufacturing in the USA, the Anna engine plant was to later move

from manufacturing GL engines alone to building powerplants for Civic and Accord cars. At Anna, all the casting, forging, machining and heat-treating processes necessary to turn raw materials into finished, sophisticated engines resided under one roof. As one associate proudly observed, 'We do what seven Honda plants do in Japan'.

The year also saw the debut of a new top-of-the-range Gold Wing. The GL1200L

1985 GL1200 Interstate, Aspencade & LE

Honda drops the standard Gold Wing in 1985, but a Limited Edition (LE) model joins the Aspencade and Interstate to mark the Gold Wing's 10th anniversary. This top-of-the-line model comes with computerized fuel injection, removable soft luggage, a Type III audio/intercom system with four speakers, cruise control, auto-levelling rear suspension and a comprehensive electronic travel computer.

Engine type:	ohc opposed-four, liquid-cooled
Bore × stroke:	75.5 × 66mm
Displacement:	1182cc
Carburation:	1.25in (32mm) CV
Starting system:	Electric
Transmission:	Five-speed
Final drive:	Shaft
Chassis:	Steel, dual shock
Front brake:	Dual disc, twin-piston caliper
Rear brake:	Single disc, twin-piston caliper
Wheelbase:	63in (1,610mm)
Seat height:	30.7in (780mm)
Fuel capacity:	4.8gal (22ltr)
Dry weight:	Interstate: 698lb (317kg)
	Aspencade: 727lb (330kg)
	LE: 350kg (770kg)
Colours:	Interstate: Metallic Silver, Metallic Blue, Wineberry Red
	Aspencade: Metallic Beige, Metallic Blue, Vintage Red
	LE: Metallic Gold two-tone
Prices:	Interstate: $6,198
	Aspencade: $7,898
	LE: $10,000

Gold Wing Limited Edition (LE) was designed to mark Honda's twenty-five years in the USA and to celebrate the tenth anniversary of the Gold Wing. Although the Aspencade had previously set the standard for luxury motorcycling, the LE raised the stakes even higher. Built to epitomize US-style touring, it wasn't just luxurious, it was festooned with gadgets and gizmos – the more the better. It was expensive too. At a list price of $10,000 it was $2,000 more than the already luxurious Aspencade. Where would it all end?

It may be difficult to imagine that the Aspencade could be further enhanced but the LE made it look basic. Although the engine was unchanged, the LE was fitted with computerized fuel injection (CFI) for the first time. This was not to improve engine performance, but rather to enhance throttle response, cold starting and fuel economy. Also, market research had indicated that CFI was something the customers wanted.

As you might expect, accessories were everywhere: there was an electronic cruise control system; an auto-levelling rear suspension system (ALRS) that maintained the pre-set factory ride heights to compensate for luggage loads; two additional pillion speakers for the stereo and running lights in the fairing lowers and panniers.

Then there was the travel computer. This was mounted at the front of the dummy tank and could calculate the bike's fuel consumption (instantaneous and average) the amount of fuel used and the quantity remaining. It could work out cruising range, trip mileage, elapsed time, and average trip speed. There was even a small map of the USA on a display that located different time zones and adjusted the on-board clock automatically.

To ask whether any of these functions were actually necessary is to miss the point – the

A new range-topper for 1985 was the GL1200LE. Despite a price of $10,000, the LE was massively successful.

Prompted by the popularity of the opulent LE, Honda introduced the GL1200SE-I for 1986.

'extras' were what set the LE apart. That and an all-up weight of 835lb (378kg) when fully fuelled.

Unfortunately, while CFI had seemed like a good idea in theory, for once the mighty Honda corporation had stumbled. Precise fuel delivery by computer monitoring of the throttle position, intake vacuum, atmospheric pressure and temperature were promised, but not delivered. The injected bikes were widely accused of rough running and poor performance. The new electronic cruise control, however, was better received.

The GL1200L was available for just one year and in one colour only – a special Sunflash Gold and Brown two-tone paint-scheme. Against all expectations (especially consider-

ing its $10,000 price tag) it was spectacularly successful and so a revised version, retailing for an extra $500, was produced for the following year – the GL1200SE-I.

Thus in 1986 there were three Gold Wings on offer once again – the now base model Interstate followed by the Aspencade and the Special Equipment model (SE-I). Common to all was revised valve timing intended to boost the mid-range power and redesigned transmission gears to reduce driveline lash. The only other change was the addition of a splashguard on the rear mudguard. The Interstate now featured a top box mounted tail-light assembly, but there were fewer colour options available with only Black joining the previous year's Wineberry Red.

1986 GL1200 Interstate, Aspencade & SE-I

The Interstate and Aspencade models can be easily identified by their new rear fender splash-guards. Otherwise, few changes distinguish the GL1200s in their third year of production. The LE is renamed the GL1200SE-I (Special Edition with Fuel Injection), and its Panasonic Type III sound system now features Dolby noise reduction. The Aspencade receives the same audio update.

Engine type:	ohc opposed-four, liquid-cooled
Bore × stroke:	75.5 × 66mm
Displacement:	1182cc
Carburation:	1.25in (32mm) CV
Starting system:	Electric
Transmission:	Five-speed
Final drive:	Shaft
Chassis:	Steel, dual shock
Front brake:	Dual disc, twin-piston caliper
Rear brake:	Single disc, twin-piston caliper
Wheelbase:	63in (1,610mm)
Seat height:	30.7in (780mm)
Fuel capacity:	4.8gal (22ltr)
Dry weight:	Interstate: 698lb (317kg)
	Aspencade: 727lb (330kg)
Colours:	Interstate: Wineberry Red, Black
	Aspencade: Metallic Beige, Metallic Blue, Metallic Silver
	SE-I: Pearl White, Beige
Prices:	Interstate: $6,698
	Aspencade: $8,498
	SE-I: $10,598

Now the middle-of-the-range model, the Aspencade's Type III radio was upgraded with the addition of a Dolby noise reduction system. Offering more colour variations than the Interstate, the Aspencade was available in two-tone Twilight Beige Metallic with Red, Pearl Marlin Blue with Spiral Blue or Trophy Silver Metallic with Tempest Grey Metallic.

The SE-I boasted all the features of the LE, most significantly CFI. There was the same auto-levelling rear suspension system

(although the SE-I's version was recalibrated with a firmer rear end setting) and like the 1986 Aspencade its Type III stereo also included Dolby. However, by weighing in at 847lb (384kg) wet, the 1986 engine developments did not make the SE-I perform any more strongly than the LE.

1987 was to be the final year for the flat-four Gold Wing. Once again, there were only two models in Honda's GL line-up – the Interstate and the Aspencade, with the SE-I consigned to history.

Both Gold Wings now had a revised drive train, claimed to reduce noise by 10 per cent. The drive shaft bevel gears were helical, rather than straight cut, and there were revisions to the damper spring and cam, as well as to the clutch and gearshift mechanism. The result was a noticeable improvement in quietness and gear selection.

After many years, Honda finally got the seat right. The new tapered seat with three-stage foam was wider for both rider and pillion with an undercut backrest in between. Additional equipment increased the bike's weight to 743lb (337kg).

The Aspencade now incorporated some of the features of the earlier SE-I, including cruise control and Type III stereo complete with handlebar controls. Its fairing was slightly changed to hide the oil filter cover and to accept auxiliary driving lights. There was also a revised ventilation system. Other features, now standard, included passenger footboards and armrests, the trunk mirror and ventilated disc brakes.

However, after thirteen years the traditional flat-four Gold Wing engine had finally had its day. During this time it had not only earned a reputation for enviable reliability, it had also come to be regarded as one of the most characterful Japanese engines ever made. Sales had exceeded 270,000, but as the years passed there had been a deepening conservatism towards the GL's development. A new age was about to dawn.

1987 GL1200 Interstate & Aspencade

The Gold Wing line-up is pared down to just two models, the Interstate and the Aspencade. Both feature a new tapered seat design with three-stage foam. The Type III sound system, passenger floorboards and armrests, and a trunk mirror are standard on the Aspencade but options on the Interstate.

Engine type:	ohc opposed-four, liquid-cooled
Bore × stroke:	75.5 × 66mm
Displacement:	1182cc
Carburation:	1.25in (32mm) CV
Starting system:	Electric
Transmission:	Five-speed
Final drive:	Shaft
Chassis:	Steel, dual shock
Front brake:	Dual disc, twin-piston caliper
Rear brake:	Single disc, twin-piston caliper
Wheelbase:	63in (1,610mm)
Seat height:	30.7in (780mm)
Fuel capacity:	4.8gal (22ltr)
Dry weight:	Interstate: 698lb (317kg)
	Aspencade: 727lb (330kg)
Colours:	Interstate: Metallic Blue, Amethyst Silver
	Aspencade: Wineberry Red, Black, Metallic Silver
Prices:	Interstate: $6,698
	Aspencade: $8,498

New Rivals

Given the Gold Wing's popularity, it was inevitable that some of its Japanese competitors would attempt to steal a slice of the market for themselves. The only real surprise was how long it took for the likes of Yamaha, Suzuki and Kawasaki to muster any kind of sustained, credible response to the big Wing. But when they came, they virtually all came at once.

The first was Yamaha's XZV1200 Venture, which was launched in 1983. An impressive machine in its own right (it forced Honda to re-engineer the GL1100 to create the GL1200 for 1984), the Yamaha had a totally different engine configuration to the Honda. Instead of the Gold Wing's flat-four, the Venture had an all-new, compact, double ohc V4. At 1198cc with four valves per cylinder (the GL had two) and four downdraught carburettors (again the GL had just two) it was capable of producing 90bhp at a time when the GL1100 could only respond with 81bhp. In tests that year it was faster than the Gold Wing both over the standing quarter-mile and in terms of outright top speed.

1987 was the final year of production for the flat-four Gold Wing, and the Wing range for that year was reduced to just two models – the Aspencade and, pictured here, the Interstate.

The first serious competition to the Gold Wing came from the Yamaha V4-powered Venture in 1983. Although a better machine than the GL1200, it never gained the same popularity and when Honda eventually launched the GL1500 in 1988, Yamaha had no reply.

The newly designed chassis made the Honda engineers sit up and take note. It boasted not only 1.5in (40mm) air-assisted forks at the front and a radical, rising rate monoshock at the rear, it also had a novel integrated braking system and together was better handling that the Wing along twisty roads. Its equipment levels were impressive too. The top-of-the-range Venture Royale, conceived to compete head-to-head with the Gold Wing Aspencade, not only offered a better sound system, it also had similar two-tone paint and self-levelling suspension.

All things considered, it was no great surprise when the Venture was chosen by *Motor-cyclist* magazine at the end of that year as the best big tourer available – ahead of the GL1100.

Also in 1983, another great rival, Kawasaki, launched its own version of the full-dresser theme – the six-cylinder ZN1300-A1 Voyager. This was the biggest and heaviest of all the touring machines, weighing in at a gigantic 829lb (381kg) with a huge 65in (1,645mm) wheelbase. However, it was this very bulk that was the Voyager's undoing. Despite an impressive peak power output of 117bhp and lavish equipment levels, including a trip computer, the Voyager was comparatively crude, ungainly and difficult to manage.

The last of the upstart rivals to emerge was, to many people's eyes, the best of all. The Suzuki GV1400 Cavalcade was launched in 1985 boasting a specification which, on paper, seemed more than a match for the enduring Wing. Like Yamaha, Suzuki also plumped for a liquid-cooled V4 engine complete with double ohcs and four valves per cylinder. Furthermore, the top-of-the-range LX model had more than enough equipment to cause a few headaches at Honda's corporate head-quarters. Features included cruise control, automatic self-levelling suspension and even an air ventilation system.

Yet none of these remarkable machines succeeded in offering anything significantly better than the Gold Wing, or had the loyal following that Honda could fall back on. As a result, none mounted a serious challenge. By 1986 the 1300cc Voyager had been replaced with a 1200cc, four-cylinder version. Though more manageable, it was never very popular

In 1983, Kawasaki launched its huge six-cylinder Voyager. Powered by the massive, liquid-cooled Z1300 engine it was the biggest of them all, but crude and ungainly too.

Suzuki, the last of the Japanese factories to try to take on Honda, launched its 1400cc Cavalcade in 1985.

although it does still survive in limited production. The Suzuki Cavalcade suffered as a result of the launch of the six-cylinder GL1500 in 1988 and was discontinued in 1990. The Yamaha Venture, probably the most successful and popular of the three, finally succumbed in 1994, unable to challenge Honda's new six-cylinder flagship – although, to Yamaha's credit, it had survived in production for ten years.

7 The Joy of Six – The GL1500

Although by 1988 the Gold Wing had seen off most of the Japanese competition, a new Wing was due. The flat-four engine had reached the peak of its development with the GL1200 and Honda, more than most motorcycle manufacturers, had long operated on the premise that 'new sells', so work began on a major revamp to the 13-year-old machine.

Predictably, Honda was cautious from the outset. Loyal Gold Wing supporters were canvassed for views and ideas about the direction a new Wing should take. The response they got was simple and to the point: more. Gold Wing owners wanted more of everything – more power, more smoothness, more features and more luxury. The new machine had to be superior in every aspect: extremely quiet and silky smooth, yet very powerful with superior handling. Honda's Japanese engineers very quickly realized that the Gold Wing they were about to create needed to extend the parameters of US touring like never before and become the definitive two-wheeled luxury platform.

It sparked the most comprehensive model development project in Honda's history, taking four years to complete. Thousands of hours were spent testing fifteen different prototype machines, and twenty different engines were routinely run near the redline for the equivalent of 60,000 miles (96,540km). The new Wing was so important to Honda they simply had to get it right.

The first parameter to be decided was engine configuration. As two of the prime goals were more power and smoothness, the obvious way to achieve this was for the new Gold Wing to have more cylinders too. It was here, ironically, that things turned full circle with a return to the flat-six engine configuration first mooted by the M1/AOK project sixteen years earlier. In 1988, the head of Honda in the USA was Soichiro Irimajiri, former M1 project leader. It is likely that this change of direction was due, at least in part, to his influence.

At the time, the M1's engine had been deemed too long for installation in a motorcycle chassis and had resulted in an impossibly flawed riding position. However, time had moved on, as had consumer acceptance of motorcycle dimensions.

Whereas the M1 had weighed in at a fairly lightweight 484lb (220kg), the new GL1500 caused amazement when it was unveiled by standing on the scales at a vast 876lb (397kg) fully fuelled. The wheelbase had been stretched out to 66.5in (1,690mm), and a capacious 6.3gal (28.6ltr) tank held the fuel. A bore and stroke of 71 × 64mm resulted in a total displacement of 1520cc but as each individual cylinder was smaller than those on the previous 1200/4, the new engine was even smoother than its predecessor. The machine's overall length was not much short of 9ft (2.75m), it had shaft drive, air suspension and, a Gold Wing first, reverse gear!

Although the six-cylinder Wing could be seen as a logical extension of everything that had gone on since the start of the dynasty back

The new six-cylinder GL1500. The legacy of the M1 was there for all to see.

in 1975, many thought Honda had gone over the top this time. The engine, now almost entirely enclosed by bodywork, provided yet more ammunition for those who regarded the Wing as nothing more than a 'two-wheeled car'. Bill Haylock, the *Bike* journalist who wrote the original 1976 article condemning the first Gold Wing for the same reason (*see* page 64) must have been wearing a very wry grin.

It is important to remember that the original GL1000 engine, although softened over the years, had been designed initially for superbike performance. The GL1500, on the other hand, was envisaged as a touring engine from the outset. The emphasis was to be on smoothness and refinement. Torque, not raw power, was the aim.

As high revs were never a consideration, there was no need for double ohcs, four valves per cylinder head or multiple carburettors and the ultimate ceiling of 5,500rpm was actually 2,000rpm lower than the GL1200. The single overhead cam, two valves per cylinder layout was retained, with the two camshafts again being driven by automotive-style rubber belts.

There was also much automotive influence elsewhere in the design. Where the previous models had predominantly motorcycle design features with just a hint of car practice here and there, the GL1500 drew far more heavily on Honda's automotive division. The gearbox, for example, featured cluster gears integral with the mainshaft, with the shifting forks mounted on a sliding dog – a design that had already been a long-term feature on Honda's cars.

Following the earlier failure of the fuel-injected GL1200, it was no surprise that the GL1500 relied on carburettors to feed its six cylinders. The carburettors were complemented by a sophisticated electronic engine management system.

The headline-grabbing 'reverse gear' was, in truth, nothing of the sort. It was actually driven off the starter motor and involved a pair of planetary gears, one for starting and one for reverse, plus an idler gear connecting the starter to the final drive gear. An interlock mechanism held the gearbox in neutral while reverse was engaged. Pulling a hand lever on the left side deployed the interlock and the 'reverse gear' engaged the final drive gear through an idler at a 660:1 reduction ratio. Keeping the starter button down saw the Gold Wing reverse at about 1mph (1.6km/h).

Several failsafe devices were employed. The 'reverse' could only be operated with the engine running, gearbox in neutral and the sidestand retracted. Transistors shut the system down if the engine stalled; a speed limiter and bank-angle sensor cut the power if the bike tipped over too far.

Computers also abounded elsewhere including more processors for the usual electronic cruise control and ignition.

Although it may sound as if the new engine and drive train were excessively complicated, and notwithstanding some gearshift 'clunkiness', they actually worked admirably.

With the emphasis on maximum low-end power, the camshaft timing was exceptionally mild, compression was only 9.8:1 and claimed maximum power was just 95bhp @ 5,000rpm – none of which was likely to set the earth on fire in 1988. But it was tractability that Honda sought with the GL1500 and in terms of torque

and sheer low-down grunt, the flat-six was a quantum leap ahead of anything else on two wheels. With a maximum torque of 110lb ft at 4,000rpm, the engine pulled cleanly and smoothly from as low as 700rpm and wound on all the way to the 5,500rpm redline.

Although the original GL1000 was universally regarded as a smooth motorcycle, and this was further improved in the GL1100 and GL1200, the new six-cylinder 1520cc unit set fresh standards of smoothness, silence and power at any speed up to the maximum of about 110mph (177km/h). Once snicked into fifth, which was effectively an overdrive, and with a fuel tank capacity in excess of 6.3gal (28.6ltr), up to 600 miles (965km) per day could be reeled off with impunity.

The sheer capacity of the GL1500 ensured that even the performance was more than acceptable. Tested in March 1988 by *Cycle* magazine, it managed a respectable standing start quarter-mile in 13.24 seconds at 97.23mph (156.44km/h). Not bad for a motorcycle designed to be anything but a dragster.

The new flat-six was a tribute to Honda's excellent design. It was only 2.5in (63.5mm) longer than the outgoing GL1200 and at 260lb (118kg) weighed just 22lb (10kg) more than its predecessor. Low-maintenance features abounded including a spin-on oil filter, an idle adjuster positioned next to the tank filler cap and a new air-cooled alternator.

The new computer-aided design-assisted frame moved away from the earlier tubular steel type and was undoubtedly influenced by the newer generation sportsbike frames such as the VFR750. The frame itself was made up of two huge rectangular box-section steel beams, running from the steering head to the swingarm pivot on to which the tubular steel front cradle and rear subframe were attached. The engine was rubber-mounted and positioned as close as possible to the front wheel for optimum mass centralization.

gear, a quieter-running helical pair was substituted for the original straight-cut gears. By putting more tooth pairs in simultaneous contact, helical gears hand off the load from one tooth pair to the next more gradual- thus controlling the noise created by bearings knocking, pistons slapping in their bores and valve tappets clicking. With liquid

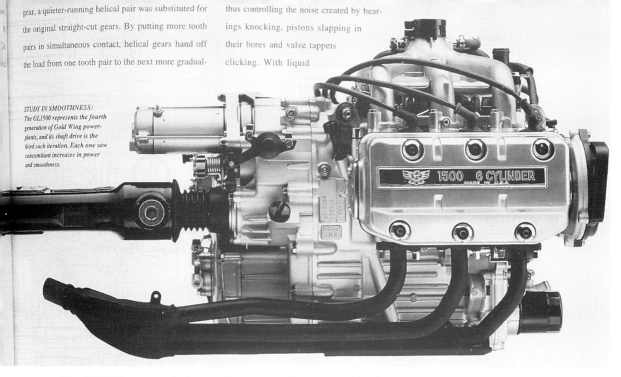

STUDY IN SMOOTHNESS: The GL1500 represents the fourth generation of Gold Wing power-plants, and its shaft drive is the third such iteration. Each one saw concomitant increases in power and smoothness.

The GL1500's new six-cylinder powerplant was not only more powerful and torqueier than the outgoing four, it was smoother too.

A new number to run alongside the Gold Wing name – but few would have imagined it would do so, so successfully, for so long.

Steering geometry was set for maximum stability with a rake of 30 degrees and 4.4in (113mm) of trail. To improve stability further, the previous 16in front wheel was replaced by a new 18-incher and a new 16in wheel was used at the rear. The front rim measured 3 × 18in (76 × 457mm) and wore a 130/70 H18 Dunlop K177 touring tyre; the rear rim, measuring 3.5 × 16in (89 × 406mm), had a 160/80 H16 Dunlop K177. Widened by

---

1988 GL1500 Standard

Honda raises the stakes again with the fourth-generation Gold Wing GL1500. The 1520cc Six sets new standards of smoothness, silence and power for the class, while the new chassis improves handling and comfort. Other new features include a unique-to-motorcycling 'reverse gear' and single-key operation of the saddlebags and trunk lids, while the bag liners are still an important luxury feature. For your listening pleasure, this Gold Wing features a 24watt AM/FM radio and stereo-cassette system with integrated intercom.

Engine type:	Liquid-cooled horizontally opposed six-cylinder
Bore × stroke:	71 × 64mm
Displacement:	1520cc
Carburation:	Two 1.4in (36mm) diaphragm-type CVs
Starting system:	Electric
Transmission:	Five-speed (including overdrive and reverse)
Final drive:	Shaft
Chassis:	Steel, dual shock
Front brake:	Dual disc with twin-piston calipers
Rear brake:	Single disc with twin-piston caliper
Wheelbase:	66.5in (1,690mm)
Seat height:	29.1in (740mm)
Fuel capacity:	6.3gal (28.6ltr)
Dry weight:	815.7lb (370kg)
Colours:	Phantom Grey, Martini Beige, Dynastic Blue
Price:	$9,998

0.5in, the wheels themselves were a new design featuring ten short hollow spokes connecting a hollowed-out hub to the rim.

The braking system was an evolution of that used on the GL1200. Again, it was a unified set-up whereby the rear brake pedal operated the right front and rear discs while the handlebar lever activated only the front left disc. All had new twin-piston calipers.

The suspension was also a development of that on the GL1200, although, after several years of relying on air springing, this feature became less important on the new GL1500. The front 1.6in (41mm) torque reactive anti-dive control system (TRAC)-equipped fork featured the same Syntallic bushings but now lacked air adjustment, while the vertically mounted rear twin shock absorbers only received air assistance on the right shock. An on-board air compressor allowed for the right shock's air pressure to be adjusted at the flick of a switch. To lower the seat height, the rear suspension travel was reduced to 3.3in (85mm), with the front forks providing 5.5in (140mm) of travel.

The result was that the new Wing handled better on the road than an 876lb (397kg) motorcycle had any right to and redefined the limits of handling and comfort for such machines. The GL1500 felt safe and secure at all times and was clearly ahead of the smaller, lighter GL1200 in handling terms.

Just one Gold Wing model, the GL1500 standard, was available in 1988 but it was a complete package provided with almost all possible gadgets. In addition to the novel reverse gear, the panniers and top box featured a clever 'central-locking' system that meant they could be opened and closed with just one key. There was also an audio system consisting of a radio with a cassette player and an integrated intercom. An electronic cruise control was also standard while the windshield was adjustable in height into three different positions.

It would be another twelve years before the new GL1500 was faced with any serious competition, and when it came – in the shape of BMW's K1200LT – it was hardly humbled.

Central to the design was the fully enclosed plastic bodywork, designed to discourage owner interference with the engine. Underneath that bodywork was surely the most complex equipment ever seen on a motorcycle, although it certainly did not detract from the Wing's reliability. The downside was when it came to servicing. Earlier Wings had not been known for easy rear wheel access. But with the GL1500, rear wheel removal almost called for an authorized Honda dealer. The huge disassembly process was illustrated in the owner's manual and required 'mechanical skill and professional tools such as a floor jack'. Not exactly the sort of equipment most riders would carry on a trip.

The huge fairing, complete with duel headlights shining through a flush fitting cover,

provided the ultimate in weather protection. Colour-matched plastic panels covered every unsightly surface, including the handlebar, and all the switches and controls were designed with style and ergonomics in mind.

Despite the digital LCD technology of the 1200cc Aspencade's instruments, Honda reverted to conventional dials with the GL1500 although between the analogue speedometer and tachometer was a rectangular LCD digital readout which displayed the time, radio frequency, and, at the push of a button, the suspension pressure.

Fuel and temperature gauges at the base of the instrument cluster were surrounded by warning lights for main beam, sidestand, low oil and fuel and an illuminated OD to warn that the overdrive ratio had been engaged.

Between the rider's knees, atop the dummy tank sits the stereo system – the volume levels self-adjust to road speed. The flap on the left is for a music cassette.

Inset into the top of the dummy tank was the radio cassette (moved from being on top of the instrument console) which was protected by a removable, lockable cover both to keep out the weather and any prying fingers.

There was a new well-padded seat (although it was no longer adjustable), while the passenger was also better catered for with a padded back, armrests and footboards. The integrated luggage system was not only easier to operate but also provided more space.

Retailing at $9,998, the new GL1500 immediately achieved everything asked of it. It rewrote the parameters for full-dress touring motorcycles and was hailed as the most significant touring machine since the original Gold Wing of 1975. *Motorcyclist* magazine voted it machine of the year and *Cycle* magazine, in a 1,000 mile test, found the GL1500 superior to all other Japanese full-dress tourers.

1988 was the final year that Gold Wings were manufactured in Japan. From 1989, all production would be in the USA. The

The word Honda is superfluous. One word says it all. Very few motorcycle models have transcended the name of their maker so strongly.

The big 15's controls and riding position are obviously an evolution of those on the 1200 but are still a triumph of development and design. A return to conventional dials made the instrumentation easier on the eye.

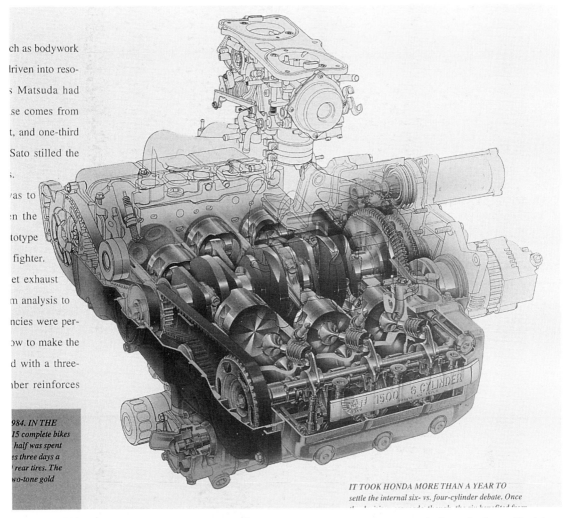

ch as bodywork

lriven into reso-

s Matsuda had

se comes from

t, and one-third

Sato stilled the

as to

n the

totype

fighter.

et exhaust

m analysis to

ncies were per-

ow to make the

d with a three-

iber reinforces

984. IN THE
15 complete bikes
half was spent
es three days a
rear tires. The
wo-tone gold

IT TOOK HONDA MORE THAN A YEAR TO
settle the internal six- vs. four-cylinder debate. Once

The 100bhp flat-six not only owes a nod of gratitude to the still-born M1 project but also owes much of its technology to Honda's car division.

models' specifications, colour options apart, remained unchanged in 1989. The only big change came in the form of a sharp rise in the retail price to $11,498.

The first and second years of GL1500 production were not entirely without their problems. There were a few complaints about the engine's sometimes jerky drive train and there was some sporadic criticism of the front brakes,

forks and cruise control, windshield adjuster and pannier seals. A few isolated clutches and ignition boxes also gave up the ghost. But the most common complaint was about the gearbox's loud clank as riders tried to shift smartly from gear to gear – a noise made all the more evident by the overall quietness of the rest of the bike.

Accordingly, there were a host of mechanical improvements to the bike for 1990 and, perhaps most significantly of all, the introduction of a second model, the higher specification Special Edition (SE).

Mechanical improvements included doubling the number of shifting dogs on the first through fourth gears to reduce driveline lash and there were also modifications to the hydraulic clutch and an increase in the gearshift lever throw. The carburation and camshaft timing were altered a touch to improve driveability and the slightly troublesome cruise control was modified. Meanwhile, the windshield adjuster was made easier to use, the forks were reworked for a smoother action and the rear suspension travel was increased a little.

The SE was introduced to mark the Wing's 15th anniversary year and was an even more luxurious machine than the standard model. This version was painted in a special 'luxury' colour (Pearl White) and was provided with an extra brake and tail-light bar on the trunk. There was also a weatherproof cover for the seat in a zippered pouch, an improved 25watt full-logic sound system, adjustable passenger footboards, warm air lower-leg vents, a vent in the windscreen for controlled airflow and illuminated handlebar switches.

The completely new GL1500 Gold Wing was the result of the most comprehensive model development project in Honda's history.

1989 GL1500 Standard

Few alterations are needed in the second year of production. The Six remains as a single model with no variants. As in 1988, options include a CB radio, saddlebag light kit, cornering light kit, colour-matched saddlebag and trunk spoilers, colour-matched lower-leg air vents, a rear speaker kit, a trunk light/mirror, and passenger audio controls. The 1500/6 badge is removed from the rear of the right-side bag.

Engine type:	Liquid-cooled horizontally opposed six-cylinder
Bore × stroke:	71 × 64mm
Displacement:	1520cc
Carburation:	Two 1.4in (36mm) diaphragm-type CVs
Starting system:	Electric
Transmission:	Five-speed (including overdrive and reverse)
Final drive:	Shaft
Chassis:	Steel, dual shock
Front brake:	Dual disc with twin-piston calipers
Rear brake:	Single disc with twin-piston caliper
Wheelbase:	66.5in (1,690mm)
Seat height:	29.1in (740mm)
Fuel capacity:	6.3gal (28.6ltr)
Dry weight:	815.7lb (370kg)
Colours:	Martini Beige, Wineberry Red, Blue Green Metallic
Price:	$11,498

1990 GL1500SE.

1990 GL1500 Standard & SE

A new Special Edition (SE) model joins the standard GL1500 and both benefit from a host of updates, including carburettor and cam revisions for better driveability and noise reduction, even tighter bodywork fit and finish, and smoother fork action. The SE sports two-tone paint, a three-position centre windscreen vent, a special rear trunk spoiler with running/brake light, adjustable passenger foot-rests, and an upgraded, full-logic sound system.

Engine type:	Liquid-cooled horizontally opposed six-cylinder		Rear brake:	Single disc with twin-piston caliper
Bore × stroke:	71 × 64mm		Wheelbase:	66.5in (1,690mm)
Displacement:	1520cc		Seat height:	29.1in (740mm)
Carburation:	Two 1.4in (36mm) diaphragm-type CVs		Fuel capacity:	6.3gal (28.6ltr)
			Dry weight:	809lb (367kg)
Starting system:	Electric		Colours:	Standard: Wineberry Red, Light Metallic Blue
Transmission:	Five-speed (including overdrive and reverse)			SE: Pearl White
Final drive:	Shaft		Prices:	Standard: $11,498
Chassis:	Steel, dual shock			SE: $13,498
Front brake:	Dual disc with twin-piston calipers			

In 1991, Honda reorganized the Gold Wing range and reintroduced the Interstate and Aspencade alongside the SE. For the first time since 1986, three Gold Wing models were available. The Interstate was to be the base model and therefore somewhat cheaper, but there was no electric reverse gear. Neither was it fitted with an on-board air compressor,

---

1991 GL1500 Interstate, Aspencade & SE

Once again the Gold Wing counts three members in its extended family, with the SE joined by Aspencade and Interstate models. The SE remains largely unchanged for 1991 except for new two-tone gold paint, and the Aspencade takes on the role of the previous standard model GL1500. The Interstate features a re-designed seat with a lower saddle height, and 40lb (18kg) less weight gives the bike a 'sportier' feel. Main items such as an air compressor, reverse gear, and saddlebag/trunk liners are not included on the new Interstate.

Engine type:	Liquid-cooled horizontally opposed six-cylinder
Bore × stroke:	71 × 64mm
Displacement:	1520cc
Carburation:	Two 1.4in (36mm) diaphragm-type CVs
Starting system:	Electric
Transmission:	Five-speed (inc overdrive and reverse, except Interstate)
Final drive:	Shaft
Chassis:	Steel, dual shock
Front brake:	Dual disc with twin-piston calipers
Rear brake:	Single disc with twin-piston caliper
Wheelbase:	66.5in (1,690mm)
Seat height:	29.1in (740mm) (Interstate: 29.5in)
Fuel capacity:	6.3gal (28.6ltr)
Dry weight:	760lb (345kg)
Colours:	Interstate: Beige Aspencade: Black SE: Gold two-tone
Prices:	Interstate: $8,998 Aspencade: $11,998 SE: $13,998

---

cruise control, top-end stereo or pannier bags. Also, the seat was higher, at 29.5in (749mm) and the windshield was not height adjustable. Weighing nearly 772lb (350kg), the Interstate was lighter than its heavier brothers, the GL1500 Aspencade, which weighed well over 793lb (360kg) and the GL1500SE, which weighed a minimum of 815lb (370kg).

Middle of the range was the Aspencade, which was equal to the former standard model, and at the top of the range, retailing at a whopping $5,000 extra and weighing 40lb (18kg) more than the Interstate, the fully loaded SE had all the goodies.

For that year all models wore commemorative '10th Anniversary' badging to mark the tenth year of production at the Marysville Manufacturing Plant (MMP) in Ohio. During this time Honda had increased its presence in the USA to seven manufacturing plants. The 1 millionth US-built Honda motorcycle, a Gold Wing of course, left the MMP production line on July 26 1996.

There were few changes to the three-model line-up in 1992, the only one of any note being that a new stereo was fitted to the Interstate. Having seen off all the competition, the GL1500 was unchallenged as the best tourer available in *Motorcyclist* magazine's best street bikes of 1992 awards.

After three years without any significant changes, there were a number of significant mechanical improvements in 1993. On all GL1500 engines the valve rocker arms now spun on needle-roller, rather than plain bearings to reduce noise and friction from the valve train. There was also an upgrade to many of the standard features, particularly so on the SE. The top-of-the-range machine now included as standard the formerly optional 40-channel CB radio and rear speakers while a left handlebar pod now controlled all the radio functions. Finally, the cruise control was now governed by the crankshaft rather than the speedometer cable, for more precise speed control.

1992 GL1500SE.

1992 GL1500 Interstate, Aspencade & SE

The big news for 1992 centres on the Interstate, which now has a revised and upgraded sound system. The Panasonic unit features a 25watt-per-channel amplifier, standard GL speakers, large and easy-to-use knobs, an intercom, a CB radio interface, a handlebar-mounted control unit, and a special input jack connector allowing the use of a portable cassette or CD player.

Engine type:	Liquid-cooled horizontally opposed six-cylinder	Rear brake:	Single disc with twin-piston caliper	
Bore × stroke:	71 × 64mm	Wheelbase:	66.5in (1,690mm)	
Displacement:	1520cc	Seat height:	29.1in (740mm)	
Carburation:	Two 1.4in (36mm) diaphragm-type CVs	Fuel capacity:	6.3gal (28.6ltr)	
		Dry weight:	800lb (363kg)	
Starting system:	Electric	Colours/Prices:	Interstate: Candy Red ($9,399), Metallic Blue ($9,199)	
Transmission:	Five-speed (including overdrive and reverse)		Aspencade: Candy Red ($12,299), Metallic Blue ($12,099)	
Final drive:	Shaft		SE: Metallic Teal ($14,199)	
Chassis:	Steel, dual shock			
Front brake:	Dual disc with twin-piston calipers			

1993 GL1500 Interstate, Aspencade & SE

All three engines now use needle bearings in their rocker-arm pivots. On the SE and the Aspencade, the cruise control reads crankshaft speed directly for more precise road-speed control. Each model comes in at least two colours, with the SE benefiting from such updates as rear-mounted speakers and 40-channel CB radio, which were previously optional.

Engine type:	Liquid-cooled horizontally opposed six-cylinder	Wheelbase:	66.5in (1,690mm)
		Seat height:	29.1in (740mm)
Bore × stroke:	71 × 64mm	Fuel capacity:	6.3gal (28.6ltr)
Displacement:	1520cc	Dry weight:	809lb (367kg)
Carburation:	Two 1.4in (36mm) diaphragm-type CVs	Colours/Prices:	Interstate: Candy Red ($9,799), Metallic Blue ($9,599)
Starting system:	Electric		Aspencade: Candy Red ($12,599),
Transmission:	Five-speed (including overdrive and reverse)		Metallic Blue ($12,399) SE: Metallic Teal two-tone, Pearl
Final drive:	Shaft		Blue two-tone, Pearl White two-
Chassis:	Steel, dual shock		tone (all $14,699); Pearl White
Front brake:	Dual disc with twin-piston calipers		solid ($14,999)
Rear brake:	Single disc with twin-piston caliper		

1993 GL1500SE.

1994 GL1500SE.

1994 GL1500 Interstate, Aspencade & SE

Honda again offers three models for 1994, Interstate, Aspencade and the SE in four colour choices each. The Interstate carries on in its role as the lightest member of the Wing family (with no reverse), the Aspencade remains the full-featured model, and the SE crowns the very top of the Wing family tree.

Engine type:	Liquid-cooled horizontally opposed six-cylinder	Wheelbase:	66.5in (1,690mm)
Bore × stroke:	71 × 64mm	Seat height:	29.1in (740mm)
Displacement:	1520cc	Fuel capacity:	6.3gal (28.6ltr)
Carburation:	Two 1.4in (36mm) diaphragm-type CVs	Dry weight:	809lb (367kg)
Starting system:	Electric	Colours/Prices:	Interstate: Candy Red ($10,199), Pearl, Dark Teal, Black (all $9,999)
Transmission:	Five-speed (including overdrive and reverse)		Aspencade: Candy Red ($13,999), Pearl, Dark Teal, Black (all $12,999)
Final drive:	Shaft		SE: Pearl Green two-tone, Pearl Teal two-tone, Candy Red two-tone (all $15,299), Pearl White solid ($15,999)
Chassis:	Steel, dual shock		
Front brake:	Dual disc with twin-piston calipers		
Rear brake:	Single disc with twin-piston caliper		

1995 GL1500 Interstate, Aspencade & SE

Engine type:	Liquid-cooled horizontally opposed six-cylinder	Wheelbase:	66.5in (1,690mm)
		Seat height:	29.1in (740mm)
Bore × stroke:	71 × 64mm	Fuel capacity:	6.3gal (28.6ltr)
Displacement:	1520cc	Dry weight:	809lb (367kg)
Carburation:	Two 1.4in (36mm) diaphragm-type CVs	Colours/Prices:	Interstate: Candy Red ($11,399), Pearl Green ($11,199)
Starting system:	Electric		Aspencade: Candy Red ($14,199),
Transmission:	Five-speed (including overdrive and reverse)		Pearl Green, Pearl Magenta (both $13,999)
Final drive:	Shaft		SE: Candy Red two-tone ($16,799), Pearl Green two-tone,
Chassis:	Steel, dual shock		Pearl Magenta two-tone (both
Front brake:	Dual disc with twin-piston calipers		$16,599), Pearl White solid
Rear brake:	Single disc with twin-piston caliper		($16,299)

1995 GL1500SE.

It was a case of more of the same for 1994, with only the colours being changed on all three Gold Wing models.

But 1995 marked the 20th anniversary of the Gold Wing and Honda was determined to do something to mark the occasion. While the GL1500 did not derive from the original GL1000, nor did it share any common parts, but it remained as the standard touring motorcycle.

In fact, by 1995, the GL1500 Gold Wing had become so dominant in its class that it had seen off all the other competing Japanese machines with the exception of the Kawasaki Voyager. Mechanical changes for the year were few. Following more customer research a further reduction in ride height came via some suspension modifications. Hand in hand with the lower seat came a lower, reshaped windscreen. The SE and Aspencade that year also received uprated top box and pannier liners, which featured leather-reinforced corners and leather carrying handles. But what set all three Wings apart for 1995 were the distinctive 20th anniversary badges on the fairing top box lid and key. Each bike even received a commemorative plaque bearing the individual machine's serial number. Honda also produced a special hard-backed commemorative history of the Wing to mark the occasion.

The Gold Wing continued to be massively popular. Despite being one of the most expensive motorcycles on the market, it was the second best-selling motorcycle in the USA during 1995, a phenomenal feat, bettered only by Harley-Davidson's entry-level 883 Sportster, a much cheaper machine.

Given this continuing success, it was no surprise that the Wing remained virtually unchanged for 1996, too, the only significant improvement being an upgrade of the Aspencade's audio system to a full-logic type that offered easier operation.

However, 1996 was also the end of an era.

It was the final year of production of the basic Interstate model, which had always proved less popular than its more lavish brothers, its production line at MMP being transferred to the Valkyrie.

The introduction of the Valkyrie led to a few more Gold Wing modifications the following year. For 1997, in addition to new handlebar switches and colours, the Wing received higher quality crankshaft main bearings, pistons, rings, valve springs, con-rod bolts and final drive gear after it was discovered that the Valkyrie's five-speed gearbox provided smoother and more precise gearshifting.

There were a few further changes for 1998. Both the SE and the Aspencade received remodelled seats, redesigned front brake covers and rocker box covers that now featured a cast '1500' emblem. The speedometer and tachometer dials, formerly black, changed to white, and the headlight and turn signal lenses were redesigned. The SE also now featured a CB radio and came in an impressive range of five different colour options.

After two years that saw the introduction of a raft of small changes, there were only very subtle changes to the Gold Wing for 1999. This was also Honda's 50th anniversary year and to mark the occasion every Gold Wing came with a special anniversary ignition key and badge on the top box and above the headlight.

It was in 1999 that the first genuine competition to the Wing for many years emerged – and it wasn't even Japanese. BMW launched the new K1200LT that year, a machine that was in many ways the first modern full-dress tourer. Although by no means without its faults, the BMW instantly made the GL1500 look almost old-fashioned. Earlier efforts by the German company to enter Gold Wing territory had been half-hearted by comparison. The fairings and luggage of bikes such as the K100LT had looked like aftermarket accessories, there was

1996 GL1500SE.

little of the plush luxury of the Wing, nor was there much of the Japanese king's solidity.

The Valkyrie (F6C)

An interesting and unexpected sub-plot to the whole Gold Wing saga came in 1996 with the launch of the astonishing Valkyrie, or F6C as it was called in Europe.

The Valkyrie was an unfaired semi-custom cruiser, based around the Gold Wing's GL1500 engine. But with a host of modifications to the engine plus a new naked roadster chassis featuring high handlebars and retro

1996 GL1500 Interstate, Aspencade & SE

The one-millionth Honda motorcycle made in the USA rolls off the MMP assembly line. Appropriately enough, it's a Gold Wing. No changes this year other then colour.

Engine type:	Liquid-cooled horizontally opposed six-cylinder	Seat height:	29.1in (740mm)
		Fuel capacity:	6.3gal (28.6ltr)
Bore × stroke:	71 × 64mm	Dry weight:	809lb (367kg)
Displacement:	1520cc	Colours/Prices:	Interstate: Candy Red ($12,099),
Carburation:	Two 1.4in (36mm) diaphragm-type CVs		Pearl Green ($11,899) Aspencade: Candy Red ($14,899),
Starting system:	Electric		Pearl Blue, Pearl Magenta, Pearl
Transmission:	Five-speed (including overdrive and reverse)		Green (all $14,699) SE: Candy Red/Dark Red two-tone ($17,599), Pearl
Final drive:	Shaft		White/Metallic Grey two-tone,
Chassis:	Steel, dual shock		Pearl Green/Dark Green two-tone, Pearl Magenta/Dark
Front brake:	Dual disc with twin-piston calipers		Magenta two-tone (all $17,399),
Rear brake:	Single disc with twin-piston caliper		Pearl White solid ($17,099)
Wheelbase:	66.5in (1,690mm)		

1997 GL1500 Aspencade & SE

The Interstate was discontinued and production capacity switched to the new Valkyrie. Otherwise, colour changes only.

Engine type:	Liquid-cooled horizontally opposed six-cylinder	Wheelbase:	66.5in (1,690mm)
		Seat height:	29.1in (740mm)
Bore × stroke:	71 × 64mm	Fuel capacity:	6.3gal (28.6ltr)
Displacement:	1520cc	Dry weight:	809lb (367kg)
Carburation:	Two 1.4in (36mm) diaphragm-type CVs	Colours/Prices:	Aspencade: Pearl Green, Pearl White (both $14,899), Candy Red ($15,099)
Starting system:	Electric		SE: Pearl Black solid ($17,299),
Transmission:	Five-speed (including overdrive and reverse)		Pearl Green/Dark Green two-tone, Pearl White/Metallic Grey
Final drive:	Shaft		two-tone (both $17,599), Candy
Chassis:	Steel, dual shock		Red/Dark Red ($17,799)
Front brake:	Dual disc with twin-piston calipers		
Rear brake:	Single disc with twin-piston caliper		

1997 GL1500SE.

styling, the new flat-six was much more than just a Gold Wing without a fairing.

Factory customs, of course, were not new to Honda. From the first 185cc Twinstar of 1978 through a family of Nighthawks, Magnas, Rebels and Shadows, customs had long been a significant part of the Honda line-up. But with the resurgence of Harley-Davidson during the late 1980s, interest in Japanese customs had waned. In 1991, to counter this trend, Honda set up an in-house think tank called 'Project Phoenix' to re-establish its

presence in the custom bike market. Although new models were the first fruits of the mission to expand Honda's custom range, it was almost inevitable that the Gold Wing too would ultimately receive the custom treatment.

Another factor influencing Honda was that by the early 1990s its plant at Anna was able to produce many more GL1500 engines than were necessary for the Gold Wing alone. The R&D department were looking to find another use for the GL1500 engine and drive

1998 GL1500SE.

1998 GL1500 Aspencade & SE	
Engine type:	Liquid-cooled horizontally opposed six-cylinder
Bore × stroke:	71 × 64mm
Displacement:	1520cc
Carburation:	Two 1.4in (36mm) diaphragm-type CVs
Starting system:	Electric
Transmission:	Five-speed (including overdrive and reverse)
Final drive:	Shaft
Chassis:	Steel, dual shock
Front brake:	Dual disc with twin-piston calipers
Rear brake:	Single disc with twin-piston caliper
Wheelbase:	66.5in (1,690mm)
Seat height:	29.1in (740mm)
Fuel capacity:	6.3gal (28.6ltr)
Dry weight:	809lb (367kg)
Colours:	N/A

1999 GL1500 Aspencade & SE	
Engine type:	Liquid-cooled horizontally opposed six-cylinder
Bore × stroke:	71 × 64mm
Displacement:	1520cc
Carburation:	Two 1.4in (36mm) diaphragm-type CVs
Starting system:	Electric
Transmission:	Five-speed (including overdrive and reverse)
Final drive:	Shaft
Chassis:	Steel, dual shock
Front brake:	Dual disc with twin-piston calipers
Rear brake:	Single disc with twin-piston caliper
Wheelbase:	66.5in (1,690mm)
Seat height:	29.1in (740mm)
Fuel capacity:	6.3gal (28.6ltr)
Dry weight:	809lb (367kg)
Colours:	N/A

2000 GL1500SE.

2000 GL1500 Aspencade & SE

Honda celebrates twenty-five years of touring excellence. No real changes this year. Wing riders are still waiting for major improvements, but what can be improved on the world's best touring bike?

Engine type:	Liquid-cooled horizontally opposed six-cylinder	Front brake:	Dual disc with twin-piston calipers
		Rear brake:	Single disc with twin-piston caliper
Bore × stroke:	71 × 64mm		
Displacement:	1520cc	Wheelbase:	66.5in (1,690mm)
Carburation:	Two 1.4in (36mm) diaphragm-type CVs	Seat height:	29.1in (740mm)
		Fuel capacity:	6.3gal (28.6ltr)
Starting system:	Electric	Dry weight:	809lb (367kg)
Transmission:	Five-speed (including overdrive and reverse)	Colours:	Candy Red/Candy Dark Red, Pearl White/Pearl Grey Green, Pearl Blue/Pearl Dark Blue, Black
Final drive:	Shaft		
Chassis:	Steel, dual shock		

train to maximize this capacity, and a plan began to form.

Makoto Kitagawa, a senior designer at Honda R&D in Asaka, Japan, drew up the first plan in 1991. His idea was to create a 'performance cruiser' with a strong Honda identity and the Gold Wing engine as the focal point. 'There were many machines with a strong American identity,' he said. 'I wanted to design an original custom using a clear Honda identity and the Gold Wing's flat-six engine is clearly identified with Honda.'

Kitagawa's first concept drawing showed a machine with early Magna styling. It also had a futuristic hydraulic drive, a chin spoiler, hidden rear suspension, and a sporty, 'bobbed' rear mudguard – very much a performance cruiser. However, it received only a lukewarm reception when shown to research groups in the USA, the prime target market. Undaunted, Kitagawa persevered. By 1992, his sketches had moved to a more retro look, which, after exploring other options, became the favoured basis for the design.

Executives, or 'associates', at Honda R&D in the USA were very clear about the route they thought the project should take. They wanted a 'hot-rod' style machine, which combined a traditional cruiser chassis with an uprated GL1500 powerplant and the wide mudguard retro look of the popular Harley-Davidson Heritage Softail.

Further sketches saw the retro look grow stronger still: flowing mudguards, a classic teardrop tank and hidden front frame downtubes. The impractical fluid drive was replaced by conventional shaft drive, and dual rear shock absorbers appeared. The engine also featured six individual carburettors. After the final sketches in 1993 and 1994, a series of clay mock-ups were constructed.

In the meantime, an early prototype had been built using a modified GL1500 chassis and engine. In trials, much of the concern about this machine centred around the sound of the engine. Although a high price Japanese mega-cruiser did not yet exist, Honda's US executives wanted a powerful, ear-pleasing growl from the electric-smooth and super-refined Gold Wing engine and constantly reminded the Japanese engineers of the sound and feel of American V8 engines by way of example.

So it came as no surprise when this early prototype failed to meet with approval. The engine characteristics were too flat, it was decided, and the flat-six engine needed livening up with more horsepower.

To achieve this, some fairly traditional hot-rodding tactics were employed. Different camshafts were installed along with six individual 1.1in (28mm) CV carburettors in place of the Wing's two. The quest for higher revs saw the return to screw and locknut valve adjusters in place of the Wing's hydraulic system. All that, combined with a new six-into-six exhaust with three enclosed into a single housing on each side, not only gave a meatier exhaust note but also boosted mid-range and peak power. Maximum power rose to 104bhp at almost 6,000rpm. And although maximum torque was slightly down on the Wing, it peaked higher at 4–5,000rpm.

Honda's design team also set about changing the whole look of the GL1500 engine. As the flat-six had originally been designed to be hidden behind acres of plastic bodywork, a visual update was deemed necessary if it was to be on show in this hot-rod incarnation.

The second prototype featured a completely new diamond-type frame, which may have looked old-fashioned but worked brilliantly. Testers claimed surprisingly good handling and the R&D bosses were so impressed that the whole programme was speeded up.

To preserve the retro look, much of the new frame had been cleverly hidden behind the teardrop fuel tank, seat and side covers. This arrangement worked well and provided

The hot rod influence is clear in the very first styling sketches for the Valkyrie – but so are carry-overs from the Gold Wing. Note the bulky wheel hubs, unstyled engine covers and single exhausts.

The first evolution of the bike's styling sees more individualism coming through. The engine covers are developing a style of their own and the exhausts are more distinctive.

128

The final styling sketch bears a very close resemblance to the finished machine. Note the flared rear fender, heavily styled engine and two-piece seat, all of which are reflected in the final article.

Using these drawings, engineers and model-makers produce a full-size clay model rendition of the Valkyrie. It is at this stage that final adjustments to the machine's look and proportions are made.

The Valkyrie in the flesh. Every inch a classic cruiser with a massive, unique engine at its heart. You'd be hard-pushed to spot the Gold Wing parentage.

From the rear the sheer size of the GL1500-derived flat-six engine starts to become apparent. Not only were cosmetic changes made to the power plant, it was completely retuned to give more lively performance, too. The first evolution of the bike's styling sees more individualism coming through. The engine covers are developing a style of their own and the exhausts are more distinctive.

The retro-look Valkyrie was launched in 1997 as a hot-rod-style cruiser based around the GL1500's flat-six engine and chassis.

The F6C badging on the tank identifies this as a European model. The US name 'Valkyrie' was deemed too inflammatory for German and Scandinavian sensibilities.

impressive stiffness. Whereas the Gold Wing used a rubber-mounted engine, on the Valkyrie it was solidly mounted. At the front end, a pair of thick, 1.7in (45mm) Showa inverted show forks were held in place by a set of equally massive aluminium yokes. At the rear was a pair of beefy Showa shocks.

In the interests of creating as much stability as possible, steering geometry was very conservative: rake was set at 32 degrees with a huge 6in (152.4mm) of trail. Rounding off the chassis components were a pair of new cast-alloy wheels, shod with specially developed Dunlop D206 radial tyres. A huge 150/80R-17 was worn at the front (as wide as the rear tyre on the 1200 Wing), while an even wider 180/70R-16 was fitted at the rear. Meanwhile, the linked braking system used on the Gold Wing was dispensed with and twin-piston Nissin calipers squeezing 11.6in (296mm) discs were fitted at the front with a single-piston caliper gripping a larger 12.4in (316mm) disc at the rear.

At over 660lb (300kg) the naked-six was indisputably heavy but at least its centre of gravity was low and the big bike was remarkably manoeuvrable at low speeds.

The riding position was less radical than it looked – by combining wide pull-back bars with conventional footpegs and control, it was actually closer to that of the Gold Wing than other customs. Because of this, long-distance travelling on a Valkyrie could be done in great comfort.

Standard equipment included a chromed, white-faced speedometer and tachometer and a huge, retro-look halogen headlamp with a multi-reflector lens.

When originally unveiled at the end of 1995, many were initially sceptical – but one short ride on a Valkyrie usually changed their minds. The vast machine's unlikely blend of style, speed and handling could not fail to impress. Honda boldly called its new creation the world's first 'performance cruiser' and few

that sampled its arm-wrenching acceleration and improbable agility disagreed.

The Valkyrie set new standards of performance for a large cruiser. Despite a wet weight of 736lb (334kg), tests for *Cycle World* magazine set a standing quarter-mile time of 12.03 seconds at 110mph (177km/h) in July 1996. The Valkyrie's top speed was impressive too, going through the timing lights at 128mph (206km/h). Compared with other big Japanese cruisers, the Valkyrie made more horsepower and provided more cornering clearance. Furthermore, despite the tuning, the 1520cc Six remained massively torquey. Honda claimed that the Valkyrie developed even greater G-forces under acceleration than its own groundbreaking sportsbike, the CBR900RR FireBlade. In short, the Valkyrie was a genuine performance motorcycle.

That impressive performance was easily exploited too. The Valkyrie pulled willingly from less than 2,000rpm, even in top gear. And with the throttle held open, the big Honda just kept on accelerating until it was storming along smoothly at 125mph (201km/h).

Nor did the Valkyrie's chassis let it down. The well-damped suspension and excellent high-speed stability made the big flat-six hugely enjoyable to ride at speed. Wide radial tyres and decent ground clearance meant the Valkyrie cornered enthusiastically and the efficient triple-disc braking system gave plenty of stopping power despite all that weight.

All in all, despite the machine's unlikely looks and surprising heritage, the Valkyrie proved to be a remarkably able, fun machine and quickly became a big success in the USA. For riders looking for a big, naked custom bike with acceleration and handling, the world's first performance cruiser was truly in a league of its own.

However, there was more to come. By 1997, the trend in big tourers was moving away from the traditional full-dress Gold Wing

Although based on the GL1500, the Valkyrie's flat-six engine was very different. On the exterior, heavily chromed and polished engine cases gave the bike a retro look; on the inside, hotter cams and different carbs and exhausts boosted peak power.

style of machine to a more traditional style. Harley-Davidson had launched its Road King; a pared-down retro tourer based on the ElectraGlide while Yamaha had come up with the Royal Star Tour Deluxe. Not wanting to be outdone, Honda launched the Valkyrie Tourer.

As its name suggests, this version came with a solidly mounted lexan windshield and a pair of colour-matched panniers, providing 35ltr of luggage capacity. It seemed set for success – when *Cycle World* magazine tested it in May 1997, the Valkyrie Tourer came out ahead of both the Harley-Davidson Road King and Yamaha Royal Star Tour Deluxe.

Despite its initial success, the Tourer was deleted from Honda's line-up three years later to be replaced by a new model – the Valkyrie

Interstate. Honda's research had indicated that customers wanted more from the Valkyrie and, following the continuing success of Harley's Road King Classic, it was time for Honda to hit back.

The engine remained as before but the Interstate had a new fork-mounted fairing, a larger 5.72gal (26ltr) tank, a more comfortable seat, a stereo system and a full-sized top box rounded off with four round tail-lights such that its rear end looked for all the world like a 50s Corvette.

It was almost as if history was repeating itself. Like the Gold Wing twenty-six years earlier, the Valkyrie had started life in a basic, unfaired form and within a few years had been transformed into the Interstate. The irony of course is that the original Valkyrie was effectively a Gold Wing shorn of all its dressings – and here they were putting them back on again!

For many, the Valkyrie Interstate proved a realistic alternative to the heavier and less powerful Gold Wing. It was less automotive, more motorcycle and with the release of the new GL1800 in 2001 the Valkyrie and Valkyrie Interstate remained the only Honda motorcycles powered by the long-serving 1520cc flat-six engine.

1996 F6C	
Engine type:	Water-cooled four-stroke flat-six
Bore × stroke:	71 × 64mm
Displacement:	1,520.3cc
Maximum power	13.3kg-m/5,000rpm
Carburation:	6 × 28mm CV
Intake system	6-carb
Transmission:	Five-speed
Clutch:	Wet multi-plates
Starting system:	Electric
Frame type:	Double cradle steel pipe
Suspension (front):	Inverted telescopic fork
Suspension (rear):	Dual conventional dampers
Front brake:	Dual disc
Rear brake:	Single disc
Dry weight:	681lb (309kg)

PC800 Pacific Coast

In a bold move to reinvent the mid- to large-capacity motorcycle in a shape that would appeal to customers with no interest in biking technology or sport, Honda created the PC800 Pacific Coast in the late 1980s. It owed much to the Gold Wing and was the result of Honda seeking to extend its automotive approach to bikes, as had been pioneered on the Wing.

When launched in 1989 it was very different to the Silver Wing, which preceded it. But the two machines had one thing in common: in many ways both motorcycles were GLs in miniature.

It was no accident that the PC800 was car-like in appearance: Honda itself dubbed it a 'motomobile' and car designs were used for inspiration for its shape. The Honda engineers sought a completely fresh approach to the traditional touring motorcycle, and had even gone as far as entrusting the bike's styling to its car division.

Underneath the all-enclosing bodywork was a rubber-mounted 800cc 45-degree V-twin that had originally seen life in 1983 in the VT750 custom. The liquid-cooled engine boasted staggered crankpins to provide perfect primary balance, chain-driven single ohcs and three valves per cylinder.

A pair of Keihin 1.4in (36mm) downdraft CV carburettors took care of carburation. As the engine was difficult to get to, maintenance-free features included a sealed battery, hydraulic valve adjusters, automatic cam-chain tensioners and a hydraulic clutch. There was also, again like the Gold Wing, shaft drive. Gold Wing-inspired design features included the frame, which had two rectangular main spars, and the underseat fuel tank. The bodywork took the enclosed look of the GL1500 one step further. Enveloped in voluptuously shaped mouldings, which incorporated sound-deadening panels, it projected a clean and smooth image, devoid of aggression.

However, in other respects the Pacific Coast differed markedly from the Gold Wing. It did not have the GL's linked brake system, using instead a conventional arrangement with twin discs and two-piston calipers from the CBR750 at the front and a single leading-shoe drum at the rear.

Not only were all the handlebars and controls hidden away behind plastic covers, but the rear end now imitated a car boot. A lid with a gas-charged shock absorber revealed motorcycle-like saddlebags.

The trunk was unlike anything ever seen before on a motorcycle – the inspirational Gold Wing included. It could comfortably accommodate four carrier bags full of groceries, or two full-sized helmets and two medium-sized gym bags. It was watertight too.

And it was comfortable, with excellent weather protection, and almost automobile-like power delivery. All told, the PC800 was an immensely practical machine.

Yet it was also an immensely heavy one. Despite weighing in at 578lb (262kg) dry, and a full 640lb (290kg) wet, the Pacific Coast was surprisingly agile due mainly to the low centre of gravity and low seat height of 30.1in (765mm). On slow corners it benefited from a good turning radius, although on faster corners it felt little mushy (the rear suspension offered four-way spring preload adjustment but the 1.6in (41mm) front forks were non-adjustable) and in a straight line the soft suspension soaked up the bumps. Testers in the USA found the PC800 to be relatively flickable, but that it tended to stand up because of its long wheelbase. It was like a Weeble child's toy: it wobbled but it didn't fall down.

The brakes were decidedly average. Fade was non-existent, but as there was not an overabundance of stopping power either, there was not much there to fade. Furthermore, the front rotors had been designed in such a way that most disc locks, annoyingly, wouldn't fit.

The 45-degree, 55bhp V-Twin was not particularly strong and had a very narrow powerband – approximately 4,500–6,500rpm. While the engine felt as though it wanted to explore the upper limits of the rpm range, its rev limiter kicked in at just after 7,000. With a lack of both high-end and low-range power, gearshifts were frequent. Top speed was close to 105mph (168km/h). Not much to write home about for an 800cc machine.

When the Pacific Coast was launched it was considered a radical bike – the world's first motorcycle to be completely hermetically sealed within an envelope of plastic, almost as if it was ashamed of its motorcycle lineage. What the Pacific Coast really wanted to be was a car, all the way down to the automobile-like instrument panel, the huge rear tail-light and the textured PVC that covered the handlebars.

The aesthetics were perhaps the most controversial element of the otherwise friendly, though bland machine. To Honda's credit, people who did not like motorcycles liked the looks of the Pacific Coast. On the other hand, traditional bikers were deeply suspicious. They were never going to look cool riding a Pacific Coast. Consequently, it didn't take off, and in 1991, after only two years, it was deleted from the Honda range in the USA (although it did make a surprising, if still fairly brief, return to the line-up between 1994 and 1998).

The PC800 was undoubtedly ahead of its time but somehow missed its mark. It was quite possibly the world's most sensible motorcycle, a station wagon of a machine at a time when adrenaline-junkie, Mountain Dew head-rush culture had replaced 'sensible and practical' with 'fast and aggressive' as objects of desire.

Just as bigger, more powerful sport-utility vehicles replaced the station wagon as the family and cargo-hauler of choice, faster, more powerful mounts like Honda's ST1100 as well as new race-bred sport-tourers like Ducati's ST2 and Honda's new VFR had sent more practical motorcycles into virtual retirement. Although fast and sporty does not always mean success in the USA (as witnessed by the surprising failure of Kawasaki's GPZ 1100 and Yamaha's GTS 1000 in recent years), all-round practicality is not what most Americans look for in motorcycles either.

Specifications

Engine type:	Liquid-cooled 45-degree V-twin
Bore × stroke:	79.5 × 80.6mm
Displacement:	800cc
Carburation:	Two 1.4in (36mm) diaphragm-type CVs
Maximum power:	55bhp/6,500rpm
Maximum torque:	48lb ft/5,500rpm
Transmission:	Five-speed, shaft drive
Wheelbase:	61.2in (1,554.5mm)
Seat height:	30.1in (764.5mm)
Fuel capacity:	4.2gal (19ltr)
Claimed dry weight:	578lb (262kg)
Measured wet weight:	640lb (290kg)

8   2001 GL1800 Gold Wing

The word 'new' does not do justice to the latest addition to the Gold Wing family, the GL1800. Two numbers alone tell of a much bigger story: 118bhp and 125lb ft of torque. There is no point in looking to find any other production bikes to compare. There aren't any. In terms of sheer grunt, the new Gold Wing is literally in a class of one. Likewise, the list of touring bikes that offer a box-section aluminium frame begins with the word 'Gold' and ends with 'Wing'. And that is only the start. Before the GL1800 was completed, Honda had ended up patenting no less than twenty technological innovations that were incorporated into this amazing motorcycle.

The development of the GL1800 is a long story. After all, how do you improve a motorcycle that, to many loyal customers, was almost perfect already? And that's the point. Honda wanted to far exceed expectations, not just to satisfy its existing customer base, but to bring in a whole new generation of riders who had yet to taste the Gold Wing experience.

There was one fundamental question to be answered before work could begin. Should they play safe by evolving the existing GL1500, so giving the Gold Wing's legion of loyal customers more to love in the way of luxury and creature comforts? Or, should they gamble with a revolutionary approach, utilizing a decade's worth of technological advances and lessons learnt in motorcycle design to chart a new course in motorcycle touring?

This posed a unique challenge for Honda's design team. While almost all motorcycle design projects take the measure of numerous competitors, the 2001 Gold Wing's designers faced just one daunting yardstick: the GL1500. The integrity of the first design was so formidable that the GL1500 ruled the world of luxury touring virtually unchallenged for twelve years.

The story of the GL1800's development began back in 1993, when work on a totally new Gold Wing began at Honda's R&D facility in Asaka. At the same time, a decision was made to put a younger engineer in charge of the project. Masanori Aoki (*see* page 161) was appointed Large Project Leader (LPL) for the new Gold Wing. However, as it turned out, finding the perfect man for the job was the easy part.

During 1994, a series of focus groups (a broad cross-section of riders, journalists and businessmen familiar with long-distance motorcycles) confirmed the direction Honda was already considering for the Gold Wing – they wanted more performance and better handling. Interviews conducted over the spring and summer of 1995 at major motorcycle rallies sharpened the concept further. Then, starting in late 1995 and continuing through early 1996, Honda mailed 23,000 questionnaires to owners of Gold Wings and other models to better quantify and qualify the direction of the new bike's development. The results were intriguing. According to Gary Christopher, senior manager, motorcycle press and motorsports at Honda America:

We began noticing a significant number of younger couples, people in their late 20s to mid 30s who really liked the level of amenities a Gold Wing provides – but wanted a motorcycle that embodied a younger, more performance-oriented image . . . At that point, we decided to see where that image would take us.

Further research brought that initial vision into clearer focus, revealing a desire for a motorcycle with traditional Gold Wing virtues such as luxury, reliability and transcontinental comfort, but with a much more powerful, 'athletic' persona. Athletic, a term chosen by Aoki's design group, became a byword for the project. Gary Christopher continues:

> That athleticism projects an image any rider can identify with, creating what Honda feels is the next logical expression of the Gold Wing ideal. You don't have to choose between luxury and high performance any more. Traditional Gold Wing customers had been amazingly happy with the motorcycle. The changes they'd like to see us make have been surpassingly simple – things like a lower seat height, less weight, new colours or adding a CD player. Therefore, it is clear that the customer looks to Honda to decide what the next Gold Wing should be. To us, that means achieving a level of comfort that has always been synonymous with the model, plus adding a much broader performance envelope and styling to match.

With the goal-posts fixed, Honda's design teams from Japan and the USA secluded themselves to focus completely on the creation of the new Gold Wing concept.

The first phase saw the creation of numerous initial design sketches. As is usual, these concept drawings varied widely as the group was given free rein to embody a design direction that emphasized power, long-distance comfort and unsurpassed reliability. However, a development theme soon emerged for the new Gold Wing design – revolution, not evolution.

Six key elements were identified to support the main design theme:

1) Prestige: a high-quality machine to uphold the Gold Wing tradition.
2) Comfort: excellent ergonomics balanced with all-weather riding comfort.
3) Function: an eye-catching design incorporating class-leading controls and equipment.
4) High-tech, high-touch: exploiting the latest technology to bring the rider closer to the motorcycling experience.
5) Individuality: a distinctive character that would embody power, fitness, strength, toughness and endurance.
6) Personalization: easy to customize to individual rider tastes.

In the first of four engineering summit meetings held in February 1997, Aoki and his team decided on the fundamental dimensions that would give shape and size to the design sketches and ideas.

Some design elements were clear right from the beginning. Since the Gold Wing had become synonymous with the horizontally opposed or flat-cylinder arrangement, the basic engine architecture was already settled. Honda considered flat-four, flat-six and flat-eight engine configurations, but when nearly all the customers surveyed expressed a preference, selected the flat-six.

The team quickly realized that the new 'athletic' persona would almost certainly call for a bigger engine – but how much bigger? They tested the flat-six arrangement in different displacements up to 2000cc. Using a heavily modified GL1500, powered by a 1657cc version of the existing flat-six, road

137

In the early stages of the design process, numerous sketches are created. In this first concept sketch note how the engine and front wheel with shrouded disc brakes, in particular, bear a strong resemblance to the outgoing GL1500.

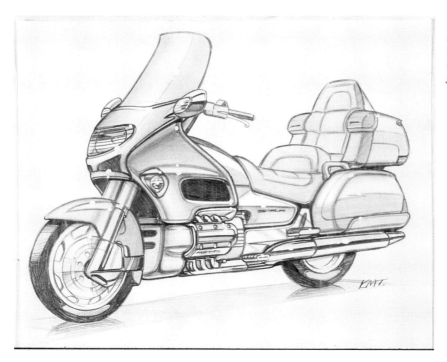

Second initial concept sketch. By now the engine has already changed form and the shrouded discs are gone.

Third initial concept sketch. The designers begin to experiment with a more curved style, complete with snub nose. Note how the engine's covers now boast '1800'.

Final initial concept sketch shows the settled snub-nose look complete with exposed disc brakes and wholly enclosed engine.

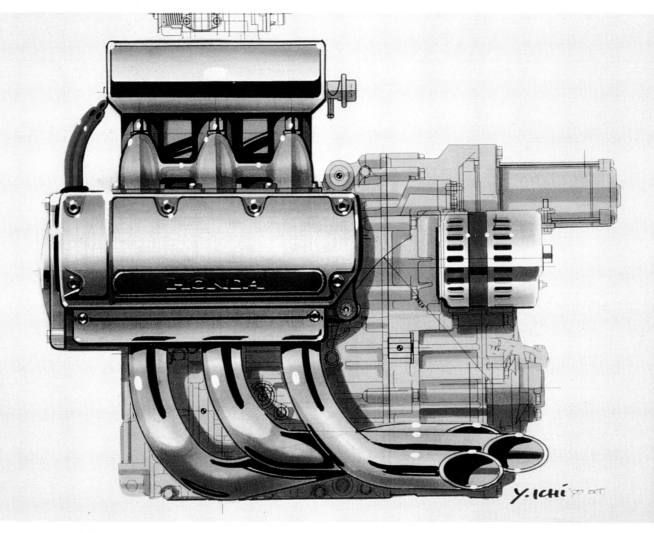

Similarly the engine itself, once all dimensions are agreed, is first depicted in a 3D drawing to determine the exact final specification.

testing began in 1997. A displacement of 1800cc seemed appropriate and, after weighing up numerous variables, an 1832cc prototype was built for evaluation in April 1999.

Despite performing with flying colours, Aoki's team was still not sure. So, in time-honoured fashion, Honda canvassed the opinions of Gold Wing owners who were asked what size they preferred – and 90 per cent of them liked the 1800.

But with the bike's displacement settled at 1832cc, there were now more difficult questions to answer. This bigger, stronger, Gold Wing engine, which was also required to be cleaner in terms of emissions, presented a veritable forest of thorny engineering problems. To make matters worse, while maintaining the same wheelbase as the GL1500, the design brief not only called for the new machine to be lighter but that it should also have more rider and passenger room. There was only one solution – to make the new, bigger 1832cc engine smaller and more compact than the previous 1500.

The solution lay in a new parallel valve train arrangement, with the intake and exhaust valves side by side to each other. This allowed engineers to slice off the bottom-rear corner of each cylinder head, creating more room for the rider's feet. The two-valve cylinder head design used direct shim-under-bucket valve actuation and required no 600 mile (965km) service. Indeed, the first valve inspection was not until 32,000 miles (51,500km).

Side-mounted radiators similar to those on the VFR800FI, VTR1000F and VTR1000R SP-2 (known as the Interceptor, Super Hawk and RC51 respectively in the USA) also helped to keep the new 1800's engine short. This in turn enabled the rider to sit 2in (50mm) farther forward in the cockpit compared to the previous GL1500, thus allowing shorter handlebars for a more direct steering feel and opening up more room at the back for greater passenger comfort.

Next in the order of business was determining the optimum power delivery for long-distance travel without exceeding exhaust emissions or fuel economy targets. With 118bhp and 125lb ft of torque, the new engine was never going to be exactly lacking in terms of character or excitement and it even met the latest California Air Resources Board (CARB) 2008 emissions standard. But Aoki was still not satisfied. So the additional targets of more defined power delivery and a free-revving character were set.

As the basic engine configuration of the 1800 was the same as that of the 1500, most of the performance gains came from other sources. First and foremost came the additional swept volume, but there was also a 50-psi high-pressure digital fuel injection system utilizing two throttle bodies and six injectors; an electronic central processor unit that pro-

vided two digital 3D fuel injection maps, and one 3D ignition map for each cylinder; and a new exhaust system with a closed-loop emission control and two exhaust catalyzers.

With the power problem solved, Aoki decided that allowing a socially acceptable amount of six-cylinder attitude to exit the Gold Wing's tail pipes was a vital part of turning up the fun factor, but this would mean minimizing engine noise elsewhere. The big three noise-producing points on the previous Gold Wing engine were the crankshaft, the AC generator and the transmission. The required noise reduction was achieved through the use of a new damper system in the generator that minimized vibration under acceleration, and recontoured gear teeth made the five-speed transmission quieter.

2001 GL1800

Engine type:	Liquid-cooled horizontally opposed six-cylinder
Bore × stroke:	74 × 71mm
Displacement:	1832cc
Carburation:	Programmed Fuel Injection (PGM-FI) with automatic choke
Starting system:	Electric
Transmission:	Five-speed including overdrive, plus electric reverse
Final drive:	Shaft
Front brake:	Dual, full-floating discs 11.6in (296mm) with three-piston calipers
Rear brake:	Single, ventilated disc 12.4in (316mm) with three-piston caliper. (ABS model available)
Wheelbase:	66.6in (1,690mm)
Seat height:	29.1in (740mm)
Fuel capacity:	6.6gal (30ltr)
Dry weight:	792lb (360kg), ABS model 799lb (362kg)
Colours:	Pearl Blue, Pearl Yellow, Black, Illusion Red

141

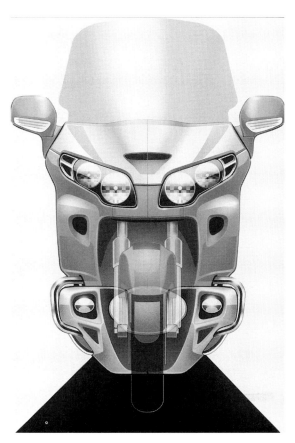

The final dimensions of the 1/8th-scale clay model are determined and confirmed. Now the creation of 3D sketches is necessary to begin both pre-development testing and the actual development of parts and assemblies.

The final 3D side-on view best shows how the new GL1800 will look. These 3D sketches will also be used to further the development of accessories.

The final 3D rear view shows how the new machine has evolved from the old GL1500. Its lines are more curvaceous, its components more integrated.

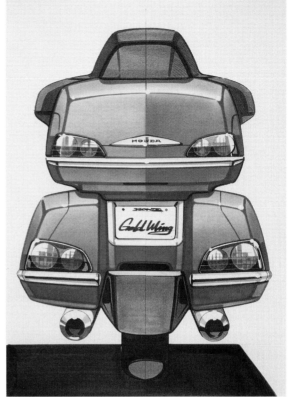

The development of the instrument console and cockpit, including the layout of all controls, is also modelled with 3D sketches at this stage. Once the final design is approved, a clay model is also created.

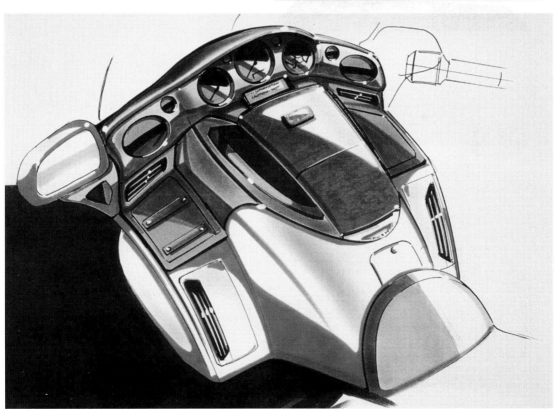

Using 3D drawings, each design sub-group created a 1/8th-scale clay model to enable further evaluation of the two designs. A skeleton base serves as a platform for the clay model.

Four months after the start of the competition, the two models are brought together for evaluation. The team that created the model with the exposed aluminium frame argues that this design best reflects the Gold Wing's powerful new engine and high-tech frame.

The second group argues for a more shrouded frame but the two teams eventually reach agreement, allowing for a portion of the new Gold Wing's frame to be exposed. Next the team needs to create 3D sketches of the winning design.

The next stage is to create a full-size clay model both of the exterior and, in the case of the Gold Wing, a complete interior model for the cockpit and instrument panel. At this stage even the surface finish is checked.

The engine too is realized in clay model form to enable designers and engineers to determine the final design.

This shows the instrument panel and cockpit rendered as a clay model to establish final specifications and dimensions.

The music centre controls are housed in a separate, easy-to-use binnacle on top of the dummy tank.

As the new engine would become a stressed chassis member, so dispensing with its predecessor's rubber motor-mounts, the 1832cc Six had to be inherently smoother. Despite the flat-six's theoretically perfect primary and secondary balance, Aoki's team reworked all the rotational balance factors inside the engine to reduce high-load harmonic vibration wherever possible. The result was the smoothest Gold Wing engine yet.

But if the powertrain was more a case of evolution than revolution, the same certainly could not be said of the chassis. Here, Aoki's

sportsbike pedigree came to the fore. It was clear to him that the new 'athletic' Gold Wing would be a perfect candidate for the aluminium technology perfected through generations of Honda Grand Prix racers, sportsbikes and motocrossers. And as with those more sporting applications, the use of aluminium opened up a multitude of options for Aoki's engineers, letting them make the new chassis light precisely where it needed to be and saving weight elsewhere whenever possible.

However, it was not without its problems.

Handlebar controls, though still daunting at first, have been refined to be simpler than ever to use.

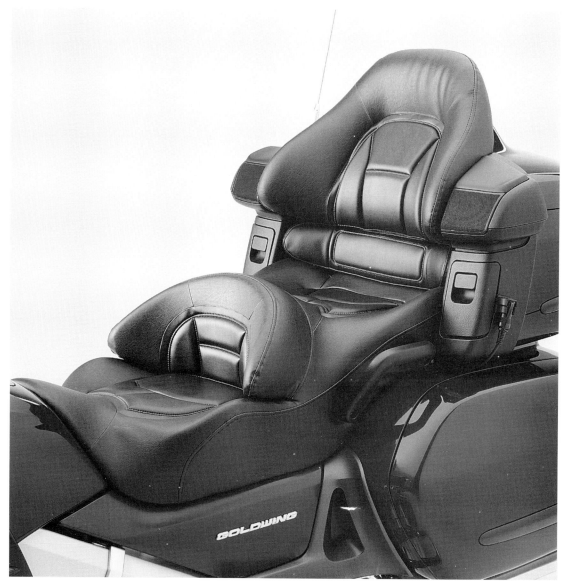

Comfort both for the rider and pillion have not been ignored – this is a perch fit for a king and queen.

The new Gold Wing's higher dynamic performance levels demanded more of key structures such as the frame and swingarm. Those demands and the limited space available made the internal frame shapes very complex. However, that complexity paid off with staggering gains in stiffness: the aluminium chassis had 119 per cent more lateral rigidity than its steel predecessor and 77 per cent more torsional rigidity.

Aoki discovered that the use of aluminium also delivered some useful manufacturing

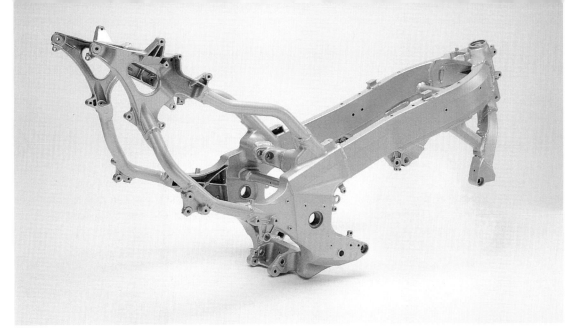

The massive extruded aluminium frame is made at Honda's Maryland plant.

ENGINE PERFORMANCE CHART

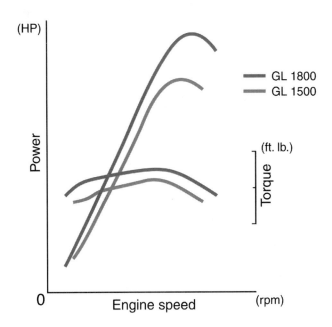

The dynograph tells the story. The new GL1800's engine is more powerful and provides more torque across the whole range than the outgoing GL1500.

advantages, enabling Honda to build multiple functions into a single component. Consequently, the dual-spar alloy frame used only thirty-one separate components, compared to the 130 individual pieces comprising the GL1500's steel frame.

Made up of multi-box-section extruded main spars and die-cast steering head, swingarm pivots and rear suspension cross-members, it was as light as it was strong, undercutting the previous steel frame by 25lb

(11.3kg). More weight savings came from the use of a single-sided 'Pro Arm' swingarm, which had the additional benefit of making a rear tyre change much simpler than before.

In January of 1998, Aoki and his team settled upon the essential chassis factors, fixing the dimensions such as steering geometry and swingarm length that would define the handling they wanted to achieve. Rake was set at 29.25 degrees (compared to 30 degrees for the GL1500) and trail at 4.3in (109mm), 0.07in

The Gold Wing has come a long way in the last three decades. Soichiro Honda himself would have been proud.

Unmistakably a Gold Wing, even from the rear – but an altogether more curvaceous and sumptuous one.

(2mm) less than the GL1500. The new single-side swingarm was shorter than the GL1500's steel unit, and the swingarm pivot was moved rearward with the object of making steering quicker, with more direct feedback for the rider.

Building athletic handling manners and supreme comfort into a 792lb (360kg) motorcycle required braking and suspension systems with unprecedented levels of sophistication, and inspired some intriguing applications of Honda technology as well as some totally new ideas.

At the front, a pair of massive 1.7in (45mm) telescopic forks housed a cartridge damper in the right leg while the left leg featured the anti-dive system, which was paired with the linked braking system (LBS). Although new to the Gold Wing, this was basically an adaptation of the systems already used on the CBR1100XX Super Blackbird and VFR800I Interceptor where servo pressure from front brake torque generates the anti-dive effect. As the right-side fork leg was not equipped with anti-dive, it could utilize cartridge-type

valving that greatly increased suspension performance. In the middle of all that sophistication, conventional dual full-floating 11.6in (296mm) front discs and a single ventilated 12.4 in (316mm) rear disc were each squeezed by triple-piston calipers.

At the back end, the Pro Arm single-side swingarm used Honda's Pro-Link single-shock system. To help absorb road shock, a unique damping system that featured a double-pipe structure with a rubber-bonded coating was applied to the drive shaft. A smaller, lighter final gearcase also helped reduce unsprung weight.

There were just as many bright ideas about the rear suspension. Honda developed an electric spring preload adjusting system. A small electric motor, activated by a switch mounted on a panel above the rider's left knee, drove a hydraulic jack-type spring preload adjuster to make rear suspension adjustments easy. A two-position memory function was then added for even easier operation.

Tyre performance was enhanced through using a new radial design that improved

Unclothed, those massive aluminium frame rails can be seen in all their glory. In the quest for more 'sporty' handling the GL1800's chassis was completely reappraised.

The GL1800 not only boasts lightweight, hollow spoke aluminium wheels but, for the first time on a Wing, Honda's Pro-Arm single-sided swing-arm suspension.

dynamic handling performance whilst main-taining the necessary long-wearing character-istics. The larger engine displacement and higher torque required more grip: a rear tyre 7in (180mm) wide with a 60 per cent aspect ratio created a larger contact patch.

Just as the physique of a world-class athlete says something of his or her abilities, so the new Gold Wing's styling had to exemplify its more athletic character – but, of course, it still needed to look like a Gold Wing.

According to American Honda's Gary

The simplicity of the GL1800's instrument console should not be confused with sparseness. The three dials are easy to read, while the central LCD digital readout gives at-a-glance information for the stereo, trip-meter and much more.

Christopher, the idea was to create a more engaging, mechanical look – less bodywork would highlight more of the bike's heart and soul:

> The riders who were interested in a high-performance motorcycle with the amenities traditionally associated with the Gold Wing wanted to see more of what made the machine tick. If the bike was lighter, it should look lighter. As a bonus, that elemental look also offers more opportunities for owners to personalize their machines with different accessories.

The design team's interpretation of that ideal took inspiration and influence from many sources. Function was as important to Aoki's team as form. For example, those side-mounted radiators were more than just racy looking – they did a better job of routing engine heat away from the rider than a conventionally mounted unit. While turn signals integrated into the mirrors are better looking, they are also more conspicuous to other motorists and more aerodynamic – the list goes on.

By October 1997, the sketches had evolved into one final list. Then, in an unprecedented step, Honda R&D in Asaka and Honda Research America both set about creating a 1/8th-scale clay model. Finally, in February 1998, an internal competition selected the best aspects of the Japanese and US designs, and a final full-scale model was created.

Honda, perhaps more than any other motorcycle manufacturer, adhered to the theory that no single facet of any motorcycle design exists in a vacuum. Thus all aspects of

Computer-aided design is used extensively in modern motorcycle design. This schematic of the frame shows the massive bracing and complex structures that comprise the swing-arm pivot area in particular.

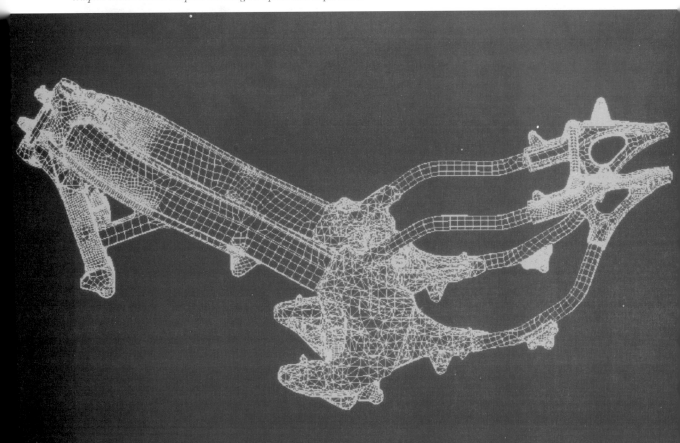

Hundreds of design sketches were eventually sorted into three key design sets labelled 'mechanical', 'conservative' and 'integrated'.

the Gold Wing were interrelated and that potential synergy was used to advantage wherever possible. The riding position on the new Gold Wing, for example, was 1.9in (50mm) closer to the fairing and windshield than on the GL1500. This had the immediate advantage of giving the rider more direct steering feel. However, by moving the rider forward, it was possible to design a smaller fairing with less frontal area and 10 per cent less aerodynamic drag, and create an additional 2in (50mm) of room for passengers. And none of that would have been possible without the

extra legroom afforded by the revised engine's parallel valve arrangement.

Because of the more aerodynamic design, the GL1800 is somewhat slimmer than its predecessor, but this is still no svelte lightweight. Air resistance of the GL1800 is about 10 per cent reduced.

Eye-catching features at the front include the large headlights, each with two 55watt halogen bulbs, and the mirrors, which incorporate the turn indictors. At the back it is the bulbous panniers and top box, each with remote-controlled central locking, which dominate. Without the extra compartment for the optional CD changer, top box capacity is 61ltr while the panniers have a capacity of well over 40ltr each.

The list of luxury features is too long to list here but some of the new highlights include: the electronic reverse 'gear' system operating from a push-button mounted on the handlebar controls; the 40 per cent response improvement in the cruise-control system; the luggage system with an impressive 147ltrs of storage and a remote control key-lock system; the state-of-the-art audio system with an optional six-CD changer; new, programmable instrumentation; and a larger 6.6gal long-range fuel tank. And the cherry on top of all that? One of the new Gold Wing's colour options is Illusion Red with 'Chromaflair' light interference pigment, a finish that alters hue as light angle and conditions change – another first for a production motorcycle.

In Europe only one model is available – the 'Standard' which comes with ABS and the Dual-CBS (Combined Braking System). But in the USA there is also a model available without the CBS-ABS brake system. The electronic cruise control and central locking (for the saddlebags, the trunk, the fairing pockets and the ignition lock) with remote control are standard features just like the so-called Honda Ignition Security System (HISS) – an ignition security system developed by Honda. Finally the windshield is adjustable in height in six different positions.

Changing the direction of a cultural icon such as the Gold Wing can be a risky business. But after employing one of the largest design teams in its history, Honda accomplished just that with the latest 1800 Gold Wing. After pouring more than seven years of effort into one of the most challenging motorcycle projects in Honda's history, Aoki and his team reinvented a motorcycle that has defined long-distance luxury riding for more than a quarter of a century. The new GL1800 possesses the soul of a sportsbike and the comfort and amenities that have always been synonymous with the legendary Gold Wing.

GL1800 Road Test Round-Up

At the previous week's press intro, I'd seen the new Wing's twin-spar aluminium frame displayed bare on a table and if someone had asked me what model it was from, I would have guessed an RC45 – it's that racy-looking. As a result, the GL1800 feels much sportier than the 1500, with a new level of tautness and steering precession. . . . Fortunately, the Wing is a veritable living room on wheels, with a La-Z-Boy of a seat and a better entertainment system than I have at home. Made by Panasonic, the six-disc changer resides in the bottom of the trunk and pops up with the push of a button.

Brian Catterson, *Cycle World*,
February 2001

Honda's new 'Wild Wing' has some serious muscle. We're talking 105.6 ft lb of torque at 4,250rpm and 97.8 rear-wheel horsepower at 5,300rpm from the fuel-injected 1832cc flat-six, surpassing the old GL1500 by nearly twenty horses and 15ft lb of oomph . . . and an unbelievably quick 1.22 second 0–30 time en route to a 12.34 second/105.84mph quarter-mile. . . . This new Wing will eat the average mega-cruiser for lunch.

Aside from acceleration, the Wing's improved handling left the strongest impression on me at the end of my One-K Day. The last few minutes of my ride were filled with sweeping bends as I crossed the Continental Divide east of Butte. If I ever again have to ride 950 miles to get in a few good curves, the GL1800 will be my sportsbike of choice.

Don Canet, *Motorcyclist*,
February 2001

US road tests rated the new GL1800 highly on its launch in 2001 – a fitting newcomer to the family.

The option of a lurid yellow paint scheme was available in the USA – as if the latest Gold Wing needed to be any more conspicuous!

Here's my 2-cents comparo between the Beemer and the Wing: Honda's new big-block is all ate up with motor and will stomp BMW's K-bike in any grunt match. Both haul ass when spun up, but the Wing rules for low-rpm lunge. The Honda's chassis is more solid, and its brakes, seat and lights are superior. The way-low seating position is more reassuring than the somewhat tippy K-bike (especially to those of us lacking a Germanic inseam), and few bikes that weigh half as much are as stable at parking-lot speeds. The flat-Six sounds cooler.

Paul Seredynski, *Rider Magazine*,
February 2001

Twist the loud handle and that ripping 1800cc Six barks great sounds, both from the intake and the exhaust. Quick, full-throttle blasts from 80 to 100 mph were invigorating, helping to break the monotony and keep my head clear. But just as nice was setting the cruise-control at 80 mph and kicking back – that silky-smooth pancake-motor as quiet as can be, making the big bike disappear like a comfortable piece of clothing.

Mark Hoyer, *Rider Magazine*,
February 2001

No other motorcycle balances this level of power, handling and braking with such luxury, comfort and convenience. Whether you're a purely long distance rider or just want more luggage space on sporty day trips, the 2001 Honda Gold Wing GL1800 is in a class by itself.

How does the Wing work when it's time to ride? In a word, the answer is marvelous, and you know I'm not given to exaggeration. In addition to the newfound power, the bike completely belies its size when you put it through the bends.

The rider's throne is wider in back, offers much more lumbar support and is well padded, yet narrows in the front to ease getting your feet down at stops and is the same height as the GL1500's. . . . The GL1800's seating position gets the rider more involved in the action, too, and it steers quickly for such a big bike yet completely remains stable at all times, even with a full load in the bumpiest of corners.

While its improved handling will only be appreciated by those who can use it, on the road the GL1800's extra power is so wonderfully useful it quickly becomes indispensable to anyone who rides the bike. . . . It revs briskly and powerfully without giving away the absolute smoothness of the old bike, and the exhaust emits a wonderful growl you have to hear to appreciate.

Mark Tuttle, Jr, *Rider Magazine*,
February 2001

Changing the course of a cultural icon such as the Gold Wing is a potentially risky business. Nevertheless, with one of the largest design teams in its history, Honda has accomplished exactly that with the GL1800. After pouring more than seven years of heart and soul into one of the most challenging motorcycle projects ever, Aoki and his team have redefined the motorcycle that has defined long-distance luxury riding for more than a quarter century. The GL1800 possesses the soul of a sportsbike, plus the comfort and amenities that have always been synonymous with the name Gold Wing.

Francis Soyer, *Popular Mechanics*,
March 2001

Although the GL1800 has approximately the same wheelbase as its predecessor, it is 20mm longer due to the new, aerodynamic bodywork. And thanks to a re-designed seat and narrower midsection, Honda claims that the 29.1″ seat height allows a rider with a 27″ inseam to touch the ground with both feet.

The Gold Wing has excellent range for a touring bike. The fuel tank holds 6.6 gallons, which provides adequate capacity to cover a good 200 miles before you go on reserve. Also well set up for travelling is the excellent hard luggage. Well-styled and integrated into the overall flow of the bodywork, they appear to be weathertight. The trunk holds 66 litres (5 litres less if you opt for the CD changer), the saddlebags hold over 40 litres each. And no matter how far you ride your new Wing in the first three years, it will remain under the warranty, which also will cover the next owner if you sell it.

John Frederick, *Motorcycle Tour & Cruiser*, April 2001

They don't get any easier than this! Honda arguably created the touring class with the 1975 GL1000, and a quarter-century later, its six-cylinder successor, the GL1500 was still selling strong. But the introduction of the Ten Best winning BMW K1200LT in 1999 forced Honda's hand and the totally new for '01 GL1800 was the result. And what a tour de force it is! With a 1832cc fuel injected flat-six engine housed in a sportsbike-spec twin spar aluminium chassis replete with a single sided swingarm, all hidden under sharp new bodywork that appeals to Gen X'ers and Preparation H'ers alike, this humdinger of a Wing scores a direct hit, and reclaims its rightful position atop the Touring Bike throne. The Wing is dead; long live the Wing!

Editorial Staff, *Cycle World*, July 2001

Masanori Aoki – Creator of the GL1800 Gold Wing

When Honda began laying the groundwork for the development of the new Gold Wing in 1993, a decision was made to put a young engineer with sportsbike design experience in charge of the project.

That man was Masanori Aoki, Large Project Leader (LPL) on the GL1800 Gold Wing. Aged only thirty-three, unusually young by Honda standards, Aoki became the LPL for the NSR250R. By the time Aoki was selected to head development of the Gold Wing, his LPL's résumé featured a number of high-performance motorcycles including the CBR250RR, CBR400RR and the CBR600F3.

Question: Why was your background in sportsbike development important?
Answer: That is the Honda way. We start by learning technology. Motorcycles have to have a sporty feeling and good handling. That's a motorcycle. Honda wanted to make the next Gold Wing like a sports model, without losing any touring capability. We set out to keep 80 per cent of the Gold Wing's touring capability. That's a vital foundation. But my job is to add a fun factor to the machine, to build a Gold Wing with the kind of acceleration and handling people normally associate with sporting machines. Even the sound is important. It's another reason you ride a motorcycle instead of driving a car.

Q: How long was the Gold Wing in development?
A: The project started in 1996. After I spent three years in the USA, I returned to Japan in 1996 on February 1. And on February 3, we started.

Q: What did you learn about culture and touring in the USA that was important to bring back to Japan for the development of this new motorcycle?
A: First, I had to learn English. Next I had to learn how people enjoyed the Gold Wing. Therefore, I went to many, many rallies. In

Project leader and the man responsible for the latest GL1800 Gold Wing, Masanori Aoki.

two years I went everywhere, and did a lot of long-distance riding. I went on a 2,220 mile trip from Anchorage, Alaska to Seattle, Washington. It's a long way between gas stations out there. I learnt how important fuel range is to the long-distance rider.

Q: Did you build in any other characteristics to the new engine to make it sportier?
A: The GL1500 engine has an electric motor quality to the power. We were after more of a motorcycle feeling. More character. More excitement. This engine [GL1800] has a lot more character in terms of a power hit, and a more free-revving character. The GL1500 engine has good power and torque, but it signs off early. You get to the rev limiter very

quickly. The new Gold Wing 1800 engine has a much more high-performance feel, especially at higher rpm.

Q: How did you arrive at the 1800cc engine size?
A: We asked ourselves what displacement is best to meet emission standards and fuel consumption, as well as optimum horsepower, torque and weight balance compared to the current model. Ultimately, it was still difficult to decide on the optimal displacement, so we asked American riders. Ninety per cent of them liked the 1800.

Q: Once you'd arrived at the optimal engine configuration, how did you decide the distance the Gold Wing should go on one tank of fuel?

A: Our original target range was 234 miles on one tank of fuel, but we're getting more than that now . . . our target was to improve fuel consumption by 30 per cent at 75 miles per hour compared with the previous engine, most of which would come from the efficiency of fuel injection. The Gold Wing FI [fuel injection] system is the same basic high-pressure design as on the CBR1100XX Super Blackbird and CBR929RR FireBlade. Ten per cent of the increased fuel economy comes from improved aerodynamics and decreased frontal area. We also added a larger fuel tank: 25 litres compared to 24 litres for the previous model.

Q: How many new technologies were developed for the Gold Wing?
A: We developed more than twenty new technologies. And all the very stringent durability standards that applied to the 1500 also apply to this 1800cc engine.

Q: Let's talk about the chassis. Why use an aluminium frame instead of steel?
A: A lot of sportsbikes have an aluminium frame because it is easier to manipulate rigidity and light weight throughout the structure than with steel. These same qualities allowed us to build the Gold Wing frame with specific strength and rigidity qualities where we needed them. Aluminium also projects a much sportier image than steel. While it was very efficient, the frame on the previous model was not beautiful. This new frame is an important part of the machine's style. Also, there is the question of manufacturing efficiency. Rigidity is very high with the new frame, and the number of parts is drastically reduced. The aluminium frame is also 25 pounds lighter than the steel frame.

Q: Now that the new Gold Wing is completed and in production, what is your goal for the marketplace?

A: My hope is that the people who buy the new Gold Wing enjoy riding it as much as I have enjoyed building it.

The New GL1800 is Born

The new GL1800 was always going to follow in the footsteps of its forebears by being built in the USA. Thus, in January 2000, with the 1800's design and development work complete, the Marysville Motorcycle Plant (MMP) in Ohio was redesigned to build the new Wing. As part of this process, the engine production line was transferred from Anna to MMP.

Ten months later they were ready to roll. In a 'line-off' ceremony flanked by four vintage Gold Wing predecessors, all assembled at the plant since the 1980 GL Interstate, and attended by hundreds of 'associates' of Honda of America Manufacturing (HAM), the first complete GL1800 rolled off the MMP assembly line on Tuesday October 10, 2000.

'The Gold Wing is a home-grown bike, with its roots right here in MMP,' said Dane Espenschied, plant manager at MMP. 'It earned its place as the first truly dependable, long-distance touring bike.'

'Our customers told us what they wanted in a luxury motorcycle – more performance. And we're providing it,' said Ray Blank, American Honda's motorcycle division vice-president. 'The new Gold Wing will set the standard for big bikes, combining legendary Gold Wing luxury with the soul of a sport-bike.'

Blank added that the timing for the new Gold Wing could not be better. Motorcycle sales industry-wide had increased by 29 per cent in the first half of the year, following several years of very strong growth. 'We are in a golden era of motorcycling and the new Gold Wing is going to capture a large share of the robust touring market.'

All-terrain vehicles (ATVs), another MMP product, had also seen burgeoning popularity.

Workers at the Gold Wing launch learnt that the plant would be producing its one-millionth ATV on Thursday, October 12, a milestone that took the associates only eleven years to achieve. Honda defined the ATV market and has remained the ATV sales leader in the USA. Now, however, much of Honda's ATV production has moved to South Carolina to allow the Ohio plant to concentrate on large motorcycles.

MMP was Honda's first manufacturing plant in the USA and when production began in 1979 there were just sixty-four associates. Today, the 700 workers at Honda's 'big bike' plant assemble models such as the Valkyrie and Shadow in addition to the Gold Wing.

There are now 13,000 workers all told at Honda of America, producing cars such as the Accord and Acura at MMP, and the Civic at the nearby East Liberty plant. Meanwhile, Honda's engine plant in Anna, Ohio produces more than one million engines each year.

Development: From Ideas to Identity

The design and development of the new 1800 Gold Wing was the biggest and most involved Honda motorcycle project ever. Not only did it cover seven years, it was undertaken by design teams working both in Japan and the USA – a first for Honda.

The 'brainstorming' phase of the process, after the basic design principles had been established, resulted in the creation of numerous initial design sketches. The eventual goal of the design group was to turn these ideas and sketches first into clay models and then into metal.

The first of four engineering summit meetings held in February 1997 enabled Aoki and his team to settle on the fundamental dimensions such as wheelbase and riding position.

The next step was to order and evolve the drawings. Hundreds of sketches were eventually sorted into three key design groups labelled 'mechanical', 'conservative', and 'integrated'. The 'mechanical' design sketches featured the least amount of bodywork and exposed the engineering internals and frame. The 'conservative' sketches closely resembled the previous GL1500 design, while the 'integrated' drawings created a more flowing shape that covered the frame and mechanical parts of the bike.

After numerous discussions and design meetings, Aoki's design group eventually narrowed their focus to two drawings from the mechanical design set. The primary difference between the two was the area of exposed frame. To display the best qualities of the two sketches, a competition was then started between two subgroups. Using 3D drawings, each group set about creating a 1/8-scale clay model to further evaluate the two designs.

A skeleton base (image 1/8-Scale Clay Model A) served as a platform for the clay model. The images on p.144 show the finishing and final inspection of the clay model whose design covers the aluminium frame.

Four months after the start of the project, the two clay models were brought together for evaluation. At this stage, the two teams compared the clay models and discussed the reasons for their particular design. The team that created the model with the exposed aluminium frame argued that their design best reflected the Gold Wing's powerful new engine and high-tech frame. Eventually a compromise agreement was reached, allowing for a portion of the frame to be exposed.

With that concept agreed the next stage was the creation of 3D sketches for the final design. First, the final dimensions of the 1/8-scale clay model were confirmed. Then the creation of

3D sketches got underway – these sketches were vital for both pre-development testing and the actual development of parts and assemblies. They would also be used to further the development of accessory parts, another vital component of the brief.

Another design team concerned itself solely with the development of the fairing cockpit – including the layout of all controls. Again, 3D sketches were produced and once the final design was approved, a clay model was created.

As is usual in the automotive industry today, 3D sketches were used in many aspects of the Gold Wing design process, as they greatly improve the speed and accuracy of development. Designing the Gold Wing was a process unlike any other on a Honda motorcycle. In some respects, it resembled the design effort required for a car. 3D sketches are used for the creation of mock-ups as well as computer-aided design (CAD) analysis. Here, these images depict the process of creating 3D sketches for the design of exterior parts such as the wheels. Similarly, the engine design depicted in a 3D sketch was also realized in a clay model form. Clay modelling allowed the team to carefully detail exterior and interior aspects of the Gold Wing, thereby improving its final production quality.

Several months later, after numerous 3D sketches and clay model components had been created, a full-size clay model of the new Wing was built – not just the exterior but a complete interior model for the cockpit and instrument panel.

At this stage, the surface finish was checked and factory team members provided input which further improved the accuracy of the 3D design drawings with an eye toward simplified manufacturing and overall production quality.

The next step was a sales meeting between the design team and American Honda's top management to check the clay model and to confirm the direction of the full-size clay design. While many detail refinements remained, an agreement was reached to proceed with a final clay mock-up model.

Several months later, the final clay mock-up was completed. In the space of just over a year the design team had completed two 1/8-scale models, a full-size clay model and a final clay mock-up – as well as the user surveys necessary to confirm the team's design direction.

Eighteen months before the new Gold Wing's launch, mock-up colours were evaluated by user surveys in Ohio and Southern California. Six months later, the design team and American Honda selected final colours. A final user survey confirmed the colours chosen.

The X-Wing – Gold Wing of the Future?

With the current GL1800 Gold Wing dominating the US full-dress tourer market and the new STX1300 Pan European V6 acclaimed as the best of the European-style big sports-tourers, it would be easy to assume that Honda has all areas of the touring market covered well into the future.

But if Honda's history has proved anything, it is that Big H never stands still and is always looking to the next generation of motorcycles. The X-Wing, a stunning prototype unveiled at the prestigious Tokyo Motorcycle Show in September 1999, gave more than a few hints as to the direction Honda was considering for its touring motorcycles of the future.

Although ostensibly designed for the European market rather than as a replacement for or successor to the Gold Wing, its style and very name suggests we may see more than a few of its facets in Gold Wings to come. Honda itself described the X-Wing thus:

> Speeding down Europe's autobahns like a wind from the Alps, this near future sports tourer is powered by an exceptionally smooth running V6 engine. Its adjustable fairing provides superb aerodynamic performance, and its elegant shape proves the maxim that form does indeed follow function. Featuring a next generation Combined Brake System + ABS, an electronically controlled Traction Control System, a multi-functional navigation system and an internet capable display monitor, and a two-way rider/pillion communication system, this machine is a showcase of state-of-the-future motorcycle technology. Safe, clean, efficient, and comfortable, the X-Wing raises tandem touring to truly new levels of elegance and performance.

It is important to remember that up to this point, luxury had always been considered to be something of a compromise in the motorcycling world. However, as the level of technology increases throughout the industry, we will almost certainly begin to see the distinction between sport-tourers and luxury-tourers slowly morph into one.

The X-Wing was built to prove this point. Aside from its striking styling, it bristles with innovation. There's the matter of the single-arm front fork-suspension – as a single-sided rear swingarm. Then there is the 1500cc, 24-valve, fuel-injected dual-overhead-cam V6 powerplant, complete with variable valve timing.

As presented, the X-Wing also had more than its fair share of electronic gizmos including traction control and automatic transmission. Rounding out the on-board electronics package are tried-and-true technologies such as Honda's Linked Braking system (LB) with the addition of ABS.

Electronic riding and comfort aids include a multi-function navigation system and a windshield that is both height and width adjustable.

At the time of the X-Wing's launch there was much public scepticism concerning some of its features, but many of these innovations are either here and accepted already or will be in the near future.

Traction control is already part of the specification of Honda's Pan European V6, while electrically adjustable windshields are familiar fare on the BMW R1150RT and Yamaha FJR1300. Automatic transmissions are now commonplace on larger displacement scooters such as Honda's 600cc Silver Wing and the Yamaha T-Max.

The V6 engine, albeit in 1100 and now 1300cc forms, has already been tried and proven on Honda's Pan European while variable valve timing made its production debut on the 2002 Honda VFR800. It is worth remembering that as long ago as the early 1980s, Honda was known to prefer the use of a V-engine in the Gold Wing and only shied away because of customer familiarity and fondness for the flat or boxer layout. Even the single arm front suspension is not radically new. In 1994, Yamaha tried (and failed) to get popular acceptance for the system with its GTS1000 sports-tourer.

If the X-Wing's system possesses the dynamic qualities of those of James Parker's design on the GTS1000, the handling and suspension performance should be exemplary, thanks to reduced stiction in the front suspension and anti-dive when on the brakes.

However, the most important aspect of the X-Wing is that all these ideas and technologies are combined into one groundbreaking package.

Sounds familiar? Remember, the original Gold Wing of 1975 was radical not for its individual technologies, despite Honda's

2001 GL1800 Gold Wing

claims. Water-cooling, underseat fuel tanks and more had all been seen before. Instead, the first Gold Wing's true triumph was combining these concepts into one radical but truly practical machine.

The X-Wing is the natural latest interpretation of that same philosophy: fascinating in detail, shockingly radical as a whole and utterly logical in purpose. It will be no surprise to see hints of the X-Wing in Gold Wings too.

Appendix
Gold Wing Accessories

One facet of Gold Wing ownership, arguably more than any other, has come to define the machine – accessories. More genuine Honda or aftermarket accessories are available for the Gold Wing than any other model on the market today. If you want everything fitting to your Gold Wing (including the kitchen sink!), you can almost certainly get it.

Here, to illustrate the range of accessories available today, is a run-down of official extras for the latest GL1800, complete with Honda's own product descriptions. Those made for the earlier models and by aftermarket suppliers are not included as they would fill another book!

Fairing Side-Air Deflectors
Aerodynamically contoured, impact-resistant polycarbonate fairing side visors with chrome-plated, corrosion-resistant zinc mounting clamps add greater wind protection.

Rear Spoiler with Brake Light
Colour-matched, impact-resistant injection-moulded ABS plastic construction incorporates a brake light and is designed to integrate with the Gold Wing's aerodynamic shape and style.

Lower Trunk Spoiler
Aerodynamically integrated, colour-matched, impact-resistant injection-moulded ABS plastic construction complements the rear spoiler with brake light for function and style.

Lower Saddlebag Spoiler
Designed to accent the lower saddlebags, these colour-matched, impact-resistant injection-moulded ABS plastic spoilers are aerodynamic and integrate with the Gold Wing's styling and shape.

Chrome Front Lower Cowl
Chrome-plated finish, injection-moulded ABS plastic lower cowl adds style and function.

Chrome Windshield Garnish
Chrome-plated finish, injection-moulded impact-resistant ABS plastic windshield garnish adds style and function.

Deluxe Removable Saddlebag Liner Set
Abrasion-resistant 1,680-denier ballistic nylon construction with leather trims. Embroidered Gold Wing icon and logo, external buttoned pocket, provides maximum saddlebag and trunk volume utilization (approximately 150ltr total capacity).

Nylon Removable Saddlebag Liner Set
Abrasion-resistant nylon construction with silk-screened Gold Wing icon and logo. Provides maximum saddlebag and trunk volume utilization (approximately 150ltr total capacity).

Trunk Net
Elastic support net firmly holds cargo in place at four points; easy installation.

Gold Wing Accessories

Chrome Sidestand
High-quality, hand-polished, double-nickel-chrome-plated sidestand.

Chrome Passenger Floorboard Cover
Chrome-finished, injection-moulded ABS plastic accents the area above the passenger floorboard with style.

Chrome Saddlebag Scuff Covers (Metal)
Contoured design offers Honda quality fit and corrosion-resistant, double-nickel-chrome-plated steel construction.

Chrome Trunk Rail
Corrosion-resistant, tubular steel rail accents the perimeter of the trunk with double-nickel-chrome-plated styling.

Chrome Saddlebag Rail Set
Corrosion-resistant, tubular steel rail accents saddlebag perimeter with double-nickel-chrome-plated styling.

Chrome Front Fender Rail
Corrosion-resistant, double-nickel-chrome-plated tubular steel contours to stylishly accent factory front fender.

Chrome Side Fairing Accents
Chrome-plated steel fairing accents install in minutes and mount directly on to the existing fairing body. Set of two (right and left sides).

Rear Speaker Set
30watt maximum output waterproof speakers integrate with the standard audio system to offer premium sound quality.

Deluxe Saddlebag/Trunk Mat Set
14oz premium quality carpet material with patch-type Gold Wing icon and logo on trunk and saddlebag mats. Mats are custom-shaped for the new Gold Wing and also feature serged edge binding and a slip-resistant polypropylene backing.

Saddlebag/Trunk Mat Set
13oz bulk continuous fibre carpet with embroidered Gold Wing icon and logo on trunk mat and Gold Wing logo on the saddlebag mats. Mats are custom-shaped for the new Gold Wing and also feature serged edge binding and a slip-resistant polypropylene backing.

Seat Weather Cover
Constructed of weather-resistant synthetic material and silk-screened with the Gold Wing icon and logo, this cover protects the seat from wet weather and the sun's damaging UV rays.

Cycle Cover
Constructed of weather-resistant synthetic material, this cycle cover features a moisture-venting system as well as a soft inner liner to prevent windshield scratching.

Front Nose Mask
Contoured to fit the Gold Wing. Constructed of high-grade vinyl material with soft inner liner and embroidered with the Gold Wing icon and logo.

Chrome Saddlebag Moulding Kit
Original factory fit, injection-moulded, chrome-plated finish ABS plastic accents the saddlebags with style.

Chrome Trunk Moulding Kit
Injection-moulded, chrome-plated finish ABS plastic accents add style to your trunk with original factory fit and finishes.

Chrome Exhaust Finishers (Turndown)
High-quality, chrome-plated steel design integrates with Honda-engineered exhaust system. Three-bolt mounting offers ease of installation.

Carbon Type Trunk Moulding Kit
Injection-moulded, carbon-fibre-type finish, ABS plastic accents trunk with a high-tech look and original factory-quality fit.

Carbon Type Saddlebag Moulding Kit
Injection-moulded, carbon-fibre-type finish, ABS plastic accents saddlebags with a high-tech look and original factory-quality fit.

Windshield (Tall)
2.08in (53.5mm) taller than the standard windshield, this polycarbonate windshield offers additional wind protection while maintaining Honda's original factory quality standards.

Windshield Air Deflectors (Standard)
Polycarbonate windshield side visors with Honda branded hardware (for standard windshields only).

Windshield (Short)
3.93in (100mm) shorter than the standard windshield, this polycarbonate windshield offers a sporty look and Honda's original factory quality standards.

Windshield Air Deflectors (Tall)
Polycarbonate windshield side visors with Honda branded hardware (for tall windshields only).

CB Antenna Kit
This CB antenna kit is specifically designed to be compatible with the Honda CB radio system and provides superior CB channel reception (use with CB radio kit).

Chrome Trunk Rack
Chrome-plated tubular steel construction is contoured to fit the trunk profile. Weight limit is 2lb (0.9kg). Note: Trunk rack will not mount with rear spoiler installed.

Index